101 GOD THOUGHTS

A Spiritual Journey from Covid to Cancer

Pete Cox

© Copyright 2024 Pete Cox

710-T Cherry Park Dr, Ste 224
Houston, TX 77095
713-766-4271

Cover design: Harvest Creek Publishing and Design

ISBN:

Dedication

This book is dedicated to the memory of my pastor, Jamie Gardner, 1966-2023. He finished his Mission with excellence and got to go home early.

Preface

This is a sort of public journal of God's dealings with me, from Covid into cancer. It contains reflections on life and love, Bible passages that grab my attention, and accounts of some of the many ways God speaks to his children— as demonstrated in my personal story.

It started for me when I was on vacation in Florida in December 2021. I was having my quiet time, and God showed me a vision of a scene from the day before, of a roller coaster I had ridden at Universal Studios. As soon as the ride started, I was in pain. All I could do was hold on and endure the ride. After showing me this scene, God impressed upon me that a big trial was coming, and I had one week to get ready. It would be like that roller coaster ride. Once started, there was no getting off. All I could do was hang on and endure it. Then He spoke to my heart and said, "Get ready." One week later I was sick in bed with Covid and had full flu symptoms. Three days later it got into my lungs, and on the sixth day I was admitted to the hospital with 74% blood oxygen saturation. The ride was well underway; all I could do was hang on.

I started posting on Facebook about my hospital experiences during those ten days I was hospitalized over Christmas and I continued writing seriously on Facebook after I went home from the hospital. At Christmas 2022, I started a blog called God Thoughts (www.PeteCox.org), and this book is an outgrowth of that blog. The blog writings continue as I proceed on my cancer journey. As I send this book to the publisher, I am currently in the hospital, getting a stem cell transplant as part of my treatment for Mantle Cell Lymphoma, a rare sub-type of B-cell Non-Hodgkin's Lymphoma. May my journey bless and encourage you!

September 13, 2023,
Medical University of South Carolina, Charleston

Contents

Introduction

"God is not a secret to be kept. We're going public with this, as public as a city on a hill. If I make you light-bearers, you don't think I'm going to hide you under a bucket, do you? I'm putting you on a light stand. Now that I've put you there on a hilltop, on a light stand—shine! Keep an open house; be generous with your lives. By opening up to others, you'll prompt people to open up with God, this generous Father in heaven." (Matthew 5:14-16 *The Message*)

We all have a journey we're on, each uniquely our own. But we can lift each other up with the wisdom of our experience to give each other hope. Pete is a husband, a father, and an entrepreneur. He's also a believer in Jesus Christ, our very real and living God. As Pete began suffering physical illnesses, he began a journal of his walk with God, and how God has spoken to his heart and helped him find hope in the darkness. This devotional is a raw, intimately real, and honest account of his daily experiences, conversations of struggle, love, and God speaking to him. This is a daily devotional book of sorts; it's also a testimony of his witness to God's grace and the reality of Jesus' living promise: "I have told you all this so that you may have peace in me. Here on earth you will have many trials and sorrows. But take heart, because I have overcome the world." (John 16:33 *New Living Translation*)

-Lauren Reeves

1. The Covid Chaplain

As some of you know, I am hospitalized with Covid. I was super miserable this morning, physically and emotionally. But God sent me someone today, and I have to tell you about it!

The hospital chaplain came in wearing just a mask (instead of mask, face shield, gown, gloves, etc.) He got a very startled look on his face when he realized I was a Covid patient, but he stayed and ministered anyway. He had done 30 years in the Army, including four combat tours. He shared his story, and then asked what I was reading. (With God in the Crucible: Preaching Costly Discipleship, by Peter Storey.) We got to talk about the book, he read some of it, and we talked about God and His dealings with us. He even told me he once met Bishop Desmond Tutu, who wrote the forward for the book. And then he prayed with me.

This man *SHOULD* have beat a hasty retreat. Unclean! That's what you do when you come across a leper. You run. Just like in *The Matrix* when you meet an agent. You run. But instead, he drew near, and ministered. What an incredible way to love a stranger. Thank you, God, for this man, who made a visible calculation to risk his life and health to be with me here.

To be Jesus to me.

2. Breathing Trouble

I lay down this afternoon to try to nap. And just like usually happens here in this hospital bed, it gets hard to breathe. It feels like my nasal passages just became restricted. It requires muscle to breathe, just like in the scary asthma attacks of my past. My heart rate jumps. My anxiety kicks in. I WILL myself to take slow steady breaths through my nose when my mind is screaming to open my mouth and breathe! Breathe fast! Hurry!

But God spoke to my heart a verse I haven't remembered since a friend wrote it into a song in December 1993 on the Anastasis, when I was away from my family in Senegal at Christmas.

> *I will lay down and sleep in peace,*
> *for you alone, Lord, make me dwell in safety.*
> *Psalm 4:8. (NIV)*

My heart slowed. I kept breathing oxygen. And my saturation came back up. Thank you, God.

3. Breath of Heaven

How I am feeling depends on my oxygen saturation at any given moment. Right now, I am resting quietly at 96% saturation and recovering from eating breakfast. Recovery from the energy required to eat a meal takes about an hour. But at 96% oxygen saturation, I am quite comfortable. A trip to the toilet (very important!) drops my saturation to about 90-92%, and then things start happening. My lungs, nose, and throat start hurting, and I start coughing. If I give in at this at this point and allow myself to get agitated instead of consciously taking deep

3

breaths, then my oxygen will drop to about 82-85% and I will totally lose it emotionally, weeping out of control. *"I CAN'T DO THIS ANYMORE!!!"* But then at that moment, if I lie prone, absolutely flat on my stomach, and breathe slowly and deeply through my nose, then my oxygen will go up to 97% again in about three minutes, and all is well...

This morning, I was having quiet time, and God brought to mind the Amy Grant Christmas song Breath of Heaven. This song never really moved me in the past, but I Googled the lyrics anyway. I mean, God brought it up, right? I got to the chorus and blinked hard.

> *Breath of Heaven*
> *Hold me together...*[1]

I was *NOT* holding it together. I am still not. But I *AM* improving physically. I want to be home with my wife. But I have to get better first. And that is *NOT* going to happen if I go home too soon.

Bottom line? All is well.

---

[1] Amy Grant. *Breath of Heaven (Mary's Song),* album Home For Christmas, 1992, track 4, Produced by Brown Bannister and Ron Huff, Sparrow Records, Brentwood TN, https://www.youtube.com/watch?v=FWo3qlqyW1c

4. Apocalypto

Early this morning I was proning and uncomfortable and trying to pray. God brought to mind an amazing scene from the movie Apocalypto. Our hero is fleeing his pursuers and in desperation, leaps over a great waterfall. As he comes out of the water, his whole perspective changes, and he turns in defiance and gives this INCREDIBLE speech:

> *"I am Jaguar Paw, son of Flint Sky.*
> *My father hunted this forest before me...*
> *My name is Jaguar Paw!*
> *I am a hunter!*
> *This is MY forest!*
> *And my sons will hunt it with their sons when I*
> *am gone.*
> *Come on!*
> *COME ON!!!"[2]*

And then God spoke Romans 8:37 to me:

> *No, in all these things, we are MORE than*
> *conquerors through Him that loved us. (NIV)*

God was gently reminding me not to have a victim mentality. I am *NOT* a victim here. I am a child of the King, and I am walking with him in *HIS* Covid Forest, and *I AM NOT AFRAID!!!*

---

[2] Apocalypto, directed by Mel Gibson (Icon Productions, 2006), https://www.youtube.com/watch?v=t1nkD2AklHE

5. Unvaccinated

Good morning friends. I am doing well. Today is day 17 of my Covid, and day 10 in the hospital on oxygen. They have me down to two liters of oxygen, and this is the best I have felt in the morning since I became ill weeks ago. I feel *GREAT*, my oxygen saturation is at 97%, and I am emotionally stable. But even feeling this good, feeling *VERY* good -- I couldn't possibly feel any better-- I still have no energy reserves. An easy bowel movement (thank God!), washing my hands, and changing my socks and underwear for the first time in days-- these *HUGE EFFORTS OF EXERTION* (I know, right?) require about 30 minutes recovery time.

And then breakfast came. I realized this morning that never in my life have I ever been truly thankful to God for food itself. I mean it tastes good, but food is usually just fuel for me. But God *BROUGHT* me this food. Not just to get me well, but to give me pleasure in the eating of it. I thank God for my food as a habit. You're *SUPPOSED* to. And as a former missionary, many times that prayer (under my breath) was "God, may this food not kill us!" Jesus told his disciples *"Eat what is placed in front of you,"* and so I did, sometimes with fear and trembling. And I rarely got sick abroad, in spite of my fears. And so this morning, I am grateful to God in my heart for my food, for the first time in my life. It was eggs, sausage, and grits. It wasn't amazing like the food my wife cooks for me. But it was for *ME*. For me here right now. In this moment. And I relished it. So, thank you God!

Now friends, I need to share my heart with you about my own Covid experience and my current thinking on the vaccine.

Many of you will want to argue with me after you read it. *PLEASE* don't. Not here. Not on my Facebook page. Message me privately, and I would be happy to talk about it at length. I am unvaccinated. And here's why. I was more concerned with the long-term risks of the new technology than I was with getting Covid. Many people in my circle had gotten Covid. Half were fully vaccinated when they got Covid. So, if they were fully vaccinated and *STILL* got Covid, why risk the vaccine? That was my thinking. But in talking with my wonderful caregivers here, they explained that, in their experience, once people get sick enough to come into the hospital, the unvaccinated have a far rougher ride. Ok, I am tough. I am 52, work out every day just by showing up at work. No problem, I can do this! Piece of cake!

But what I didn't really understand is what "high risk" really means. Certain people are high risk. People who have asthma (me) diabetes, smokers, or are fat. There, I said it, and I'll not take it back. For whatever reason, Covid seems to really relish going after people who are overweight. Something about fat cells. I don't know, I am not a doctor. But being overweight makes you high risk. It is what it is. Anyway, I thought warnings about being "high risk" meant you had a higher chance of getting Covid. But, for most of my friends and family, getting Covid was an annoyance. Some just lost taste and smell. For my teenagers, it wasn't as bad as the cold we passed around a few months ago. For others, it feels like the flu. I have had the flu twice. I wanted to *DIE*. But I got through it. And the first week of Covid hit me exactly like the flu. Like a mule! Fever, chills, sweats, nausea, vomiting, extreme joint and body pain. It sucked, but it's just pain. And then it attacked my lungs, and that is where it actually got scary.

I had been thinking that me being high risk (thank you God I am not a smoker!) made it easier for me to get Covid, so, social distance, etc. If I get it, I will deal with it, and get on with life.

But what I understand now is that, if you are high risk and you *DO* get Covid, *AND* you get sick enough to end up in the ER, *AND* you are unvaccinated… this is going to *KICK YOUR BUTT!*

And so, my friends, my thinking has changed. I still believe there are risks to the vaccine. I do. I know people who have reacted badly. But I personally believe the reward of my body being better able to fight this off is worth the long-term risks. I am sick *NOW*. God will deal with tomorrow, just like he is walking with me today. My daily life is filled with risk. It's my job. If my wife spent a week at work with me, she would never sleep again. It's fine. Risk is part of life. Actually, faith is spelled R-I-S-K! (Thanks Steve Meeks!) So for me right now, for where I am, I have decided to take the vaccine in the future. They tell me I need to wait a couple of months, and that is fine.

This Covid journey is my own. I wanted to share my experiences with you because I hope it helps someone. Each of you will have to make your own decisions on the vaccine, because it's *YOUR* life, and *YOUR* health. Therefore, it must be YOUR decision. This is where I am at. So sue me. I love you guys, and I deeply appreciate all the love you have shown me in this process. God bless you. [**Author's Note:** I never did get vaccinated, and now have no plans to do so.]

6. How to Pack for the Hospital

Good morning friends. All is well. I realize some of you have sick loved ones, or perhaps you yourself are contemplating going to the hospital and the Planner in you is desperately wondering what to pack! Let me share a little of my perspective. I only brought a change of underwear and my toothbrush, but my wife has been sending me care packages and I am now well equipped! Here are things that I have either found helpful, or wish I had thought of before this morning:

1. A *SMART* phone, not a flip phone. Many of us have aging parents who have a flip phone and don't like to text. It's just too much work! But listen. This is *REALLY* important. Communication with family is going to be the biggest morale booster. And if they have Covid Pneumonia like I got it, physically talking is exhausting. I am good for 5 minutes, 10 minutes MAX, and then I start crashing. So while I *WANT* to talk with my family, I just can't. Texting is the workaround. With group texts, you can update everyone at once. Or you can have private conversations. Download a texting app. I use Facebook Messenger and Telegram. But seriously, teach your people how to text, how to do phone apps, how to do video calls, how to live as a modern. This is huge. (I know your father is grumpy. Too bad. Make him learn.) A smart phone is a tool. A weapon. He needs to be proficient in the use of this weapon. *TOUGH* love, people! Also, load a Podcast app. This will give freedom of choice about what to listen to. I personally *DESPISE* TV news, because most of it is about stuff I just don't care about, and it makes me impatient. But my wife has been teaching me about podcasts, and now the freedom

of choice is refreshing! My current favorite is Young Heretics, by Spencer Klavan.

2. Pajamas! (And warm socks.) They will give you a hospital gown. It opens at the back. And if you have Covid, you absolutely MUST be sleeping on your belly. Which means your gown flops open, and your bare skin is exposed. You have a blanket, sure. But the air is ALWAYS blowing. And when you're hooked up to a finger oxygen sensor, a heart monitor, and maybe even an IV and lying on your stomach, you personally are not capable of covering yourself in the night, so you're going to get cold. BUT... if you bring comfortable pajamas... (I have been wearing very comfortable long underwear for 11 days-- it's the best!) If you bring comfortable pajamas, then you will sleep better, everyone won't be seeing your wobbly bits every time they walk in the room, and life is just... better. Also, pack your favorite zip-up hoodie, and some T-shirts. I often find that I struggle to keep my body temperature regulated. But by switching back and forth between my T-shirt, my long underwear, and my hoodie, I can manage. Just barely at moments, but I am managing. My room has a thermostat, but it is programmable and refuses all my efforts to override it. I am COLD. It is blowing cold air. And there is absolutely NOTHING I can do that will make it stop. At the moment, my room is 69.7 degrees, even though I tried to set it at 87. Nope! But with three types of clothing in my arsenal here, I am able to cope. Just plan for it.

3. Something to occupy your mind. A book perhaps, or three. A notebook and pen. A Bible. Something that you enjoy doing when all alone. Because you are going to have a LOT

of alone time. And TV is just... boring. Pack reading glasses!

4. A toilet kit. Toothbrush, toothpaste, razor, deodorant. All your medications. Now, they won't let you *TAKE* your meds from home, but they really want to see the bottles themselves to see what you're on. I shaved Christmas morning for the first time in a week and a half. It was my Christmas gift to myself. Self-care is a thing. Feeling good about yourself is healing.

5. Butt cream! For diaper rash. Hahahaha! Yeah, I know. They will give you baby wipes, which is wonderful, but over time those may irritate your tender bottom. (I'm just being real here people, nobody get excited.)

6. Food items. They will always be bringing you ice water, but when your lungs are coated with mucus, you need a *HOT* drink to loosen it, not a cold one. So pack herbal tea bags. Ask for hot water as soon as you wake up, and with every meal, and drink it! For me, these tea bags have been huge in making me feel decent at any given moment. Also, many of you have food addictions-- to hot sauce. Your food is going to come with salt, pepper, and maybe butter. So if you are into Tabasco sauce, pack a bottle! Also, things like candy and baked goods. Little memories of home, but they will make you *FEEL* good. *SCREW* the calories, *EAT* that brownie!! They will give you steroids, and towards the end you will be ravenous. Like the Marvel movie character Venom, prowling for food. *"HUNGRY!!! HUNGRY!!! HUNGRY!!!"* Having snacks from home will help you cope until the next meal comes. Also, as your body ramps up to fight the Covid, your metabolism is going to get *JACKED*,

and you will want to eat double or triple what you normally do. It's normal. Don't stress. Eat the food. Eat all your vegetables. It will help you heal and that's why you're here. Coffee! I love having coffee when I wake up. Except, I am waking up at 5 am, and breakfast doesn't come until 8:30. I wish I had thought of bringing instant coffee and creamer from home so I can make it in the early morning.

Anyway, I hope you found this helpful, or at least amusing. Thanks for being here for me.

7. Respiratory Anxiety

All is well. I want to share with you this morning my struggles with respiratory anxiety. I grew up with asthma, and there were a number of specific moments when I had a massive asthma attack, usually brought on by allergies, and I was caught without my inhaler. It got bad enough that it required conscious thought and deliberate muscle action to breathe. *"BREATHE IN!!!"* [suck] *"BREATHE OUT!!!"* [blow]. Terrifying. And then in 4th grade at summer camp, I made the decision to take a scuba lesson. There in that pool, having to use muscle to activate the regulator totally triggered me and I had to get out of the pool.

I should also say that I nearly drowned as a young child. I was walking along a lake shoreline in chest-deep water and stepped in a hole. I saw my father look up, yank off his boots, and come charging in after me. He grabbed me by the hand and lifted me out of the water. (Thanks, Dad!) (Incidentally, when your kids are at the pool, WATCH them. Don't play with your phone. *WATCH* them.) My parents gave me swimming lessons after that, and I am a good swimmer now. I did the mile swim in Boy Scouts and earned the Life Saving Merit Badge. But even now, I don't like being in water where I can't touch the bottom, or where I must swim underwater. I can use a snorkel, but I take zero pleasure in it. The opposite in fact. And often I have to swim for work. A timber piling may get loose, fall off my barge, and start floating away. And then I have to swim for it. *("That thing cost $600! Get in there!")* It totally sucks, but that's the job.

So here in this hospital room, there have been many scary moments, especially in the early stages, when I would be feeling great! And something would happen and my energy reserves would be used up without warning. My blood oxygen saturation would start falling, my lungs would start hurting, it would suddenly get harder to breathe, and *ALL* these old memories would hit me like a fire hose. My heart rate would *SPIKE*. "I'm dying!!!" From all-is-well to sheer terror, usually in less than 30 seconds. But then I learned that if I start proning – lying flat on my stomach – and breathing *SLOWLY* and *DELIBERATELY* through my nose and oxygen tube, then I *WILL* get air, *I WILL* be able to breathe, my oxygen saturation will come back up, and my lungs will stop aching so badly. It takes about 2 minutes. That's all! And if I keep lying there and *DELIBERATELY* breathing slowly, my lungs will feel warm inside, and I will feel good, and be ready to get back in my chair.

"Breath of Heaven
Hold me together..."

(Thanks, Amy Grant.) And so in talking about my panic with an old friend, she shared something amazing with me from her own life and agreed that I could share it with you.

> *Yes, I know that terror. It took time and I had a couple of very good pulmonary doctors explain that the feelings of anxiety were a physiological response (not just a psychological one). It was part of my body's alarm system to let me know – "hey, something's wrong!" Or "my brain or other organs are not getting super-charged oxygenated blood... better take it easier and make sure they get some!"*

> *It may seem weird to be grateful for strange body responses (especially when you're in the midst of it and your body isn't cooperating and it feels so very bad!) but I learned to be grateful- for the tachycardia, breathlessness, dizziness, nausea, etc. – all those things I hated (and still reeeaaallly DON'T like) because if I didn't have those "early warning systems" I would probably regularly pass out without warning or who knows what!*

> *One of hardest things you have to do now is be patient with yourself and allow healing in God's time. I won't tell you it will be easy... I don't know what the future holds for you, only the Lord does. My best advice for you as you walk through this journey (from the hard-learned lessons of my own) ... Instead of focusing on what God "can do" (and whether*

He is or isn't doing it), I learned much by
focusing on WHO God IS. The Psalms are so
awesome for that... He is a shelter, a shepherd,
a savior, a strong tower, etc.

Learning about this *NORMAL* physiological response was good for me. I imagine people with chronic anxiety-- not me normally-- may think of themselves as weird. Not normal. Different. Like something is wrong with them. Something broken inside. And I imagine that must be emotionally debilitating at times. But what if... what if in *SOME* of these times, you are Normal? What if this is just your body warning you, just like if you stick your hand over a candle flame. That pain? That's your body warning you to *STOP DOING THAT!!!* And so in this case, this spike of anxiety is just my body prompting me to get more oxygen. Don't be alarmed. Nothing to fear here...

And so my friends, thanks for listening. Maybe somebody needs to hear this today. You're not strange. You're not weird. You're normal, at least in this aspect. And that's ok. Whatever you are struggling with, God has *GOT* this. And God is a *VERY* good listener. So talk with Him about it. Write Him a letter maybe. And message me too if this helps you. I would love to hear back from you.

8. Recalled to Life

I had been, (in the words of A Tale of Two Cities, by Charles Dickens) "Recalled to Life." They wheeled me out of the hospital where I had spent Christmas with Covid, and into the waiting arms of my wife. She took me home and took good care of me.

This wasn't how Christmas was supposed to go. We were planning to spend Christmas with my family in Virginia. Instead, we had our first and only family phone call during my hospital stay on Christmas Eve. It was a Friday night, as I recall. I had entered the hospital the previous Saturday and was at the two-week mark with my symptoms. I think this one was a video call (and I *LOATHE* video calls, but decided this was the one time to make an exception.) By about the 7-minute mark, I was coughing too badly to continue. We said goodbyes and signed off. I cried pretty hard that night. On Christmas morning, my wife took the kids to their grandparents in Virginia, then went home to wait. I don't think we spoke on the phone again for days, but we texted a lot. My eventual homecoming was sweet, but I had rough days (weeks?) ahead. Still, God sustained me.

As I think about it, I had definite plans for Christmas week and the following ones. But everything had to change. I survived the experience, but it was a good lesson to hold things lightly. Tomorrow is not guaranteed. Do you love someone? Tell them. Are you estranged from family or friends? Fix it. Do you have a dream vacation to an exotic location in the back of your mind? Book that ticket. Have you always wanted to learn to dance? Check out www.RevolutionBallroom.com, and just do it. Been engaged for years? Just get married already! Having the perfect wedding is overrated. BEING married to someone who loves you-- THAT'S the stuff!

> *For all of the most important things, the timing always sucks. Waiting for a good time to quit your job? The stars will never align, and the traffic lights will never all be green at the same time. The universe doesn't conspire against you, but it doesn't go out of its way to line up all the pins either. 'Someday' is a disease that will take your dreams to the grave with you. Pro and con lists are just as bad. If it is important to you and you want to do it 'eventually,' just do it and correct course along the way.*
> *- Timothy Ferriss, The 4-Hour Workweek*[3]

So, New Year's Resolution time is coming up. How about instead of resolving to lose 20 lbs., resolve to fix broken relationships. To make amends. To celebrate the people in your life. To have the experiences you've been postponing. To develop the closeness with God you've been longing for.

---

[3] Timothy Ferriss, *The 4-Hour Work Week: Escape 9-5, Live Anywhere, and Join the New Rich* (New York: Random House, 2009)

9. Darted!

I have been home for nearly 24 hours, and some of you have been asking how it's going. The scene in Despicable Me 2 where Lucy shoots Gru's obnoxious date with a dart gun explains it pretty well! I will be feeling good – great even! And then, it's like someone *DARTS* me with moose tranquilizer, and suddenly I'm down! Suddenly, as in 15-20 *SECONDS*. And now I can't lift my head enough to point it at the TV. I am utterly immobile. This condition may last three minutes, or three hours. There is absolutely no predicting it. And then, as though a light switch is thrown, I am better. Phenomenal even! As though it had never even happened...

Switches seem to be a theme for me right now. Either my lungs *HURT* and I am coughing and weeping from the pain... or they don't. And then I don't even feel them. They're just doing their job. Then this morning, I got hit by massive upper back pain. It felt like heavy pressure, like I imagine a heart attack would feel like. Except it was just on my back and not my chest. I begged my wife for pain meds and jumped into a hot shower. Right as she arrived, the pain was gone. It was just like turning off a light switch. All these transitions take place at lightning speed, with pretty much zero warning. It's annoying.

It also hurts my pride because I treasure my independence. I would like to be able to drive myself somewhere – to the store maybe, or to see a customer, but I can't. I might have a random episode and would never make it off the road in time. So I sit here in my chair. [Sigh.] This morning, a young mom friend with a toddler and a newborn asked me how I was doing and what my recovery plan was. I told her I didn't have one, because... I can't do anything but sit here. So the plan is to sit here. Read. Journal. Pray. Chat with friends. Just... *BE* for a while. (Incidentally, I am being waited on hand and foot, while she is about to lose her mind with everything demanding her immediate attention, and *SHE* is asking how *I* am doing?) Wow. It's like being fish-slapped!

This morning I shaved my head. I last did that Christmas morning. This simple act, shaving my head with a razor and shaving cream, took 3-5 minutes. But it took absolutely everything out of me for hours. I am feeling good at this precise moment, and am so grateful to God for my bride, who loves me so much, and who is taking such incredible care of me. And I am thinking of a great quote I saw:

> *"We are not called to see through each other,*
> *but to see each other through."*

Do you know someone who is struggling? Who is barely holding it together? (Or maybe they're not?) Don't just pray for them. Pitch in. Come clean their kitchen. Fold their laundry. Take their baby to the park so they can take a nap or finally have sex and reconnect with their spouse. Make them a meal. Pitch in. Don't just talk about Jesus. *BE* Jesus to them. Like the chaplain who accidentally wandered into my Covid room and *STAYED*.

See each other through.

10. Self-Care for Young Moms

I know some young moms. And some moms who aren't quite so young, but who have young children. And they are *FRAZZLED*. They remind me of a moment from my brother's wedding when my wife was trying to sing a solo. Our son (age 3?) wriggled out of his grandmother's grasp, ran down the aisle, and made a beeline for my wife. He clung to her dress, and started in.

> *"Mommy? Mommy? Mommy? Mommy?*
> *MOMMY? MOMMY? MOMMY! MOMMY!!!"*

Cool as a cucumber, my bride touched her fingers to his lips to calm him, and just kept singing.

And that's what you do. You just keep singing. But you also practice some self-care. Frazzled mom, here is a sample recipe to try for self-care. I made it up myself, so if it doesn't work, you can yell at me:

1. Get up, meet your child's immediate needs. Diaper, medicine, food. (Actually, maybe not food. Maybe just set out some cheerios and let them fend for themselves.)

2. Take a bath or a shower. (Now listen. This is not about presentation, so you don't look unkempt for your partner. This is for *YOU*.) Some of you haven't showered in four days because you have little kids, and you are drowning! But stop yourself. Turn the TV on. Another ten minutes of screen time won't hurt their development, I promise. *LOCK THE BATHROOM DOOR*. I can't emphasize this enough. *("Mommy? Mommy? Mommy? Mommy?")* Now take your bath.

Take a steam shower. Play your favorite songs on speaker. Revel in this little luxury. Because you need this. Honestly. Oh, and that baby that started crying for you at the door as soon as you sat down in the tub? They're just going to have to deal. Mommy is unavailable.

3. Put on a little makeup, *IF* you like how you look with makeup. This is about feeling good about yourself, and this is a small accomplishment that will make you *FEEL* better about yourself.

4. Put on "real clothes", not pajamas. Nothing fancy. "Walmart-Wear" I call it. If you would wear it to Walmart, then that's good enough. But putting your pajamas back on suggests you are going back to bed, and you are not! Because that's what depression makes you *WANT* to do- to just go to bed. So you fight it by getting dressed.

5. Make the bed. Doing this takes two minutes max, but it does several things. It gives you a sense of accomplishment. Do you like check-boxes? I do. And I confess, sometimes I will throw an extra item onto my list, something super easy, just to have the gratification of checking it off. It's almost cheating, but it works for me. Making the bed is like that. But more importantly, now that the bed is made, you don't want to mess it up by going back to bed and taking all those pillows back off. Too much work. So later today, you may get down. You might feel depressed. And you are going to look at the bed and just want to escape there. I see you. But you

have stuff to do, so you need to bump that for now. So make your bed. You will thank me later.

6. Make coffee. *COFFEE!!!* (I am reminded of a Christmas recipe I saw for Best Rum Cake Ever. The recipe starts out with "First, sample the Rum. *GOOD, isn't it?*") Hahahaha! Yeah, it's like that for me too. (I see you.) Honestly, I do this step absolutely first. But I have that luxury because my kids are grown. Actually, because I am impatient, my first cup (or three) is from *YESTERDAY'S* pot of coffee because I can throw creamer in, pop it in the microwave, and be drinking it a minute later! You know, as opposed to the *excruciating* 10-minute wait it takes to brew a fresh pot? Priorities people! So I nuke the first cup, and then maybe start a fresh pot. Nah, who am I kidding? I drink the old coffee to the dregs and *THEN* make a fresh pot. Mustn't be wasteful! So, you do you! Figure out your best coffee routine, and then drink it like a boss.

7. Retreat. As in getaway. Solitude. A place with no kids. Find somewhere in the house where you can be by yourself for 10 minutes. (Remember, the kids are still parked in front of the TV and that is *GOOD* parenting. Don't let anyone tell you otherwise.) So retreat to somewhere quiet and alone. Bring a Bible. Bring a notebook. Bring your pen. Bring your coffee. You are going to write a letter! To God.

(Blink)

Yeah, I said it. Sit yourself down and write a letter to God.

Thursday, December 30, 2021

Dear God,

It's me again...

Tell Him what's bothering you. Tell Him what you're excited about. Tell him about what's going on with you. Tell him stuff. Whatever comes to mind. Get it all on paper as you sip your coffee. Now open your Bible and read. It doesn't matter where, really. God knows what you need. Just read a bit. And if a particular passage really grabs your attention, copy it down on the letter you just wrote. Take notes. Then write to God some more. Do you remember how you first really got to know your partner? You spent time together. You just hung out together. And you talked a lot. That's all this is, really. Hanging out with God for a few minutes. And you need this.

8. Check on the kids. (**Helpful Hint:** They're *FINE*.) Moving on!

9. Do a little cleaning. Not a *LOT* of cleaning, I said a little. And *ONLY* a little. Because this is about self-care, not about being Wonder Woman. Your whole place needs cleaning, I get it. The kitchen is trashed, there are clothes all over the floor in the bedroom, you haven't done laundry in days, and a cyclone's aftermath of toys litters the floor. I get it. But the idea of cleaning the *WHOLE* house is depressing. So you're going to break it down. First, throw a load of laundry in the wash and let it run. Second, empty the dishwasher. Third, walk

away... (I can see it in your eyes now, that haunted look. *"Are you freaking kidding me? Have you seen this PIT?"*) Yup. Now walk away. An empty dishwasher is a necessary accomplishment, and just the right amount of work done to feel good about yourself. This afternoon, you can load the dishwasher, but not now. Just walk away. You're done here.

10. Check on your kids and shift back into Mom Mode. You have done your self-care, now start your day.

11. Proning

Can I share something cool? I had a verse on my heart this afternoon. It was Psalm 4:8:

> *I will lie down and sleep in peace,*
> *for you alone, O LORD, make me dwell in*
> *safety.*

I couldn't remember the reference, and I was flipping around for it and found this verse, the page before, Psalm 3:5.

> *I lie down and sleep;*
> *I wake again, because the LORD sustains me.*

Okay, nice, nice. These were in *The New International Version*. The *NIV*. But here's the really cool part. Here is how *The Message* phrases it:

> **I stretch myself out. I sleep.**
> *Then I am up again- rested, tall and steady..."*

Oh my goodness! This is a description of Proning! When I was in the hospital and fighting for air, they taught me Proning. If you lie flat on your stomach and bring your arms up, something about this position stretches your lungs out, and gives you maximum oxygen absorption. When I am in respiratory distress, if I stretch myself out this way, I start feeling better in minutes.

> *I stretch myself out. I sleep.*
> *Then I'm up again- rested, tall, and steady..."*

Proning. Wow God!

12. New Year's

I was thinking tonight about my future and stressing a little to God about it in my journal. In response, He spoke John 14:27 *(NIV)* to my heart, before I could even finish scratching out the sentence:

> *Peace I leave with you; My peace I give you. I*
> *do not give to you as the world gives. Do not let*
> *your hearts be troubled, and Do Not Be*
> *Afraid[!]*

Okay God. Thank you God.

13. Love and Risk

All is well. I'm hurting some, but each day is a little easier, and I went for my first walk yesterday. I am cogitating this morning on the link between love and risk. This passage in Matthew 28:16-17 in *The Message* totally intrigues me:

Meanwhile, the eleven disciples were on their way to Galilee, headed for the mountain Jesus had set for their reunion. The moment they saw him, they worshipped him. Some though, held back, not sure about worship, about risking themselves totally.

Wow. They were having an actual *PHYSICAL* "mountain top experience" with the risen Christ, and *STILL*, "some held back, not sure about worship, about risking themselves totally." I have a former pastor, Steve Meeks, who liked to say "Faith is spelled R-I-S-K." I totally believe that. But I also believe that love is spelled R-I-S-K. Sara Groves wrote an amazing song a while back, called Loving a Person:

'Loving a person just the way they are
It's no small thing
It takes some time to see things through
Sometimes things change sometimes we're
waiting
We need grace either way.

Hold on to me I'll hold on to you
Let's find out the beauty of seeing things
through

There's a lot of pain in reaching out and trying
It's a vulnerable place to be
Love and Pride can't occupy the same spaces
baby

Only one makes you free
Hold on to me..." [4]

Sometimes, the people we love hurt us. It's how it is. And it sucks. But the proper response is to love anyway. In the book *The Velveteen Rabbit,* Margery Williams makes the same point in a slightly different way:

> *It was the Velveteen Rabbit who asked the Skin*
> *Horse (who "was so old that his brown coat*
> *was bald in patches and showed the seams*
> *underneath, and most of the hairs in his tail*
> *had been pulled out.")*
>
> *"What is REAL?..."*
> *"Real isn't how you are made," said the Skin*
> *Horse. "It's a thing that happens to you. When*
> *a child loves you for a long, long time, not just*
> *to play with, but REALLY loves you, then*
> *become Real."*
> *Does it hurt?" asked the Rabbit.*
> *"Sometimes," said the Skin Horse, for he was*
> *always truthful. "When you are Real you*
> *don't mind being hurt."[5]*

[4] Sara Groves and Gordon Kennedy, Loving a Person, album Add to the Beauty, track 12, produced by Brown Bannister, INO Records/Fair Trade Services, Brentwood TN, 2005, https://www.youtube.com/watch?v=UmBSYNf9V3o

[5] Margery Williams, *The Velveteen Rabbit* (New York: George H. Doran Company, 1922)

I have a favorite love quote. The author is unknown, but it has been going around Instagram and I think it is perfect:

> *The truth is that the more intimately you know someone, the more clearly you'll see their flaws. That's just the way it is. This is why marriages fail, why children are abandoned, why friendships don't last. You might think you know someone until you see the way they act when they are out of money, or under pressure, or hungry, for goodness' sake. Love is something different. Love is choosing to serve someone and be with someone in spite of their filthy heart. Love is patient and kind, Love is deliberate. Love is hard. Love is pain and sacrifice. It's seeing the darkness in another person and defying the impulse to jump ship.*

I really love the ending. "Love is pain and sacrifice. It is seeing the darkness in another person and defying the impulse to jump ship." You people who are dating think *LOVE* is moonlight and roses, and it's *NOT*. It's daylight and dishes and crying babies and surly teenagers. It's Commitment. If you are together long enough, you *WILL* hurt each other. Stick it out. Love anyway. Love through the pain. Don't run. Love them. Work it out. R-I-S-K.

14.   Let the Waters Roar

I would like to introduce a book to you, *Let the Waters Roar: Evangelists in the Gulag*, by Georgi Vins. It is a collection of stories of Christians in the Soviet prison system. I believe their stories are still relevant today, as we still serve the same faithful God.

As I was in my hospital bed, God showed me a storm. I was in the water, churned by the waves. God has been talking to me for some time about a Storm coming, and my thought on seeing the waves was, "Well, I'm in it now!!!" And then I recalled *THIS* story, *THIS* testimony, and I wanted to share it with you:

> *When my family lived in Kiev, we were given a*
> *large, beautiful painting. On it was portrayed a*
> *raging sea, tempestuous clouds, and large*
> *waves pounding against enormous stones and*
> *cliffs. The picture was in a handsome frame.*
> *But the most important thing about the painting*
> *was the words written on the dark background*
> *of the sky and waves, excerpts from the first*
> *three verses of Psalm 46:*
>
> *God is our refuge and strength...*
> *Therefore we will not fear... though the waters*
> *roar!*
>
> *In March, 1974 I was arrested, and in January*
> *1975 I was brought to trial in Kiev. The public*
> *prosecutor charged me with nine accusations,*
> *all of them religious theme, including*
> *preaching the gospel and printing Bibles. The*

29

court sentenced me to five years deprivation of freedom in strict-regime labor camps plus five years of exile. On top of that, they handed down a third penalty: the confiscation of all personal property! This punishment was intended to hurt my family...

Soon after the trial, I was transported to one of the labor camps near the city of Yakutsk in Siberia. Sometime later, during a visit to the camp, my family told me how confiscation of property had proceeded. When the sentence went into effect, a special commission had arrived at our house to take inventory for confiscation: the table, the chairs, the buffet, a bookshelf, the couch, the washing machine, the refrigerator, dishes, and so on. The commission even decided to confiscate the painting on which was written "God is our refuge and strength... Therefore we will not fear... Though the waters roar!

The full name of the painting was entered into the record, which made the commission reluctant to have custody of something glorifying God like this!

Then he turned to Ivan Petrovich. "As I understand it, you're also a believer?"
"Yes, I also believe in God, who is our refuge and strength!"

"Maybe you'll buy this painting from the government?" the official asked. Then he

30

pointed to the document and the furniture and said, "All these confiscated objects already belong to the government. We can sell the furniture and painting to anyone we want. Buy this painting from us! What are we going to do with it? We don't need this painting. We won't ask much for it. Just five rubles!"

Ivan Petrovich pulled five rubles out of his pocket and presented it to the commission. Next, taking the painting, he triumphantly hung it on the wall in its original spot and loudly read, "God is our refuge and strength... Therefore we will not fear... though the waters roar!".

And so this painting remained in our house, proclaiming the strength and might of God, and encouraging and comforting the hearts of many believers persecuted for faith in Christ who visited our home in Kiev." [6]

---

[6] Georgi Vins, *Let the Waters Roar; Evangelists in the Gulag.* (Grand Rapids: Baker Book House, 1989), 9-13.

15. Fear

Hey everyone. God has been nudging me about fear lately. Some time ago, I was stressing over something unimportant, and He showed me an infant perched on his father's mighty arm. His father was making a muscle and supporting the baby behind its back with his huge hand. I'm talking Dwayne "The Rock" Johnson level of muscles. Anyway, the infant was doing a "startle" reflex, *CLINGING* to his father's mighty arm for dear life, as though it was the baby's job to hang on tight enough not to fall! When really, he could have spread his hands wide, and let go. Because his father was holding him against his chest, firmly and securely, and that frightened infant wasn't going anywhere. His father was cradling him in his mighty arm, and he didn't need to panic.

16. Mr. Clean

As I was lying in bed this morning, God showed me Kojak. Or perhaps it was Mister Clean. An older man, like me, shaved bald (also me), but *TOUGH*. And... muscular! I immediately started thinking. "Wow God. I need to start working out again. Join a gym or something." And then I remembered my big workout yesterday. I drove myself to Walmart and then CVS, and that GREAT WORKOUT (Ha!) totally did me in. I was done for the day! Ridiculous. Then this thought of my current condition really started to get me down. But then God played the chorus of the song Jireh for me, by Elevation Worship:

Jireh- You are enough
Jireh- You are enough
I will be content
In every circumstance
Because Jireh-- You are enough![7]

God was telling me that this weakness, this relative helplessness, this DEPENDENCE on others-- was where HE has placed me for this season, and I need to roll with it. To trust Him. To be content.

Yes God. Thank you God.

17.   Marco Polo

Did you know Marco Polo encountered the Christmas story in his travels in Persia? Well, read on! I discovered *In the Footsteps of Marco Pol,* by Dennis Belliveau and Francis O'Donnell while sitting in the library on our cruise ship a couple of years ago. Here are a couple of excerpts:

> *PREFACE*
> *...In the spring of 1993, when Fran and I were*
> *both around 30 years old... We had taken it*
> *upon ourselves to try, "in the most literal*
> *sense," to put Marco Polo's journey on the*
> *map.*
> *Perhaps the two are inseparable, but with a*
> *dash of reckless bravado and a lot*

---

[7] Elevation Worship and Maverick City Music, *Jireh,* album Old Church Basement, 2021, Sony Music, Nashville TN.

*of testosterone, we set out on our mission to see
as many places Polo described without
resorting to aircraft. We have tried to keep the
story you are about to read "in the moment,"
and aside from a few historical updates, the
words have come directly from the journals
kept during the two years we were gone."*

On page 263, they are now in Persia-- modern day Iran. And
suddenly, in this devout Muslim country, they encounter the
Christmas Story!

*"We came upon a town of fire worshipers...
The inhabitants here told me that in days gone
by three kings set out from this country to
worship a new-born prophet and took with
them these gifts-- gold, frankincense, and
myrrh."*

- Marco Polo

The authors explain:

*For over twelve hundred years, the fire burning
in the Zoroastrian temple in Yazd has been kept
alive by a long lineage of priests, log upon log
and ember to burning ember.*

*The ancient Zoroastrian religion is perhaps the
first monotheistic faith. Centuries before
Christianity, the Zoroastrians believed that
their God would send a savior, born of a virgin,
to triumph over darkness and evil. Great
astrologers, the Magi of Persia, also believed
that the sign of his birth would come from the*

heavens. Their veneration of fire as a sacred channel of God's eternal light and purity is still practiced by a small group of followers in Iran today." [8]

WOW! Did your jaw drop from reading that? Mine did. A Savior, born of a virgin, and the sign of his birth would come from the heavens...

Have you ever wondered about the ancient Christmas carol, We Three Kings? I always puzzled over the quantity because the Gospel accounts never quantify the number of magi. I had always assumed the number three was traditional because there were three gifts-- gold, frankincense, and myrrh. But now I wonder, was it from Marco Polo talking about his visit with the Zoroastrians in Persia? I wonder...

18. The Crossroads

Just before Christmas a year ago, God gave me a dream in which I came to crossroads. The path to the left was beautifully paved, winding through a butterfly meadow. Birds were singing, and there was even a rainbow! But the path to the right? That was a hard path. It led steeply downhill and into a dark and scary forest, much like Mirkwood from The Lord of the Rings. Also, the path itself? Terrible. Full of rocks. A difficult descent. Nope, Nope, Nope! But in the dream, Jesus was standing at the crossroads, and reaching out His hand to

---

[8] Denis Belliveau and Francis O'Donnell, *In the Footsteps of Marco Polo.* (Lanham, MD: Rowman & Littlefield Publishers Ltd, 2008), viii, 263-264.

walk with me down the hard path and into the forest. But it was clear in the dream that I was free to choose...

The next morning, I was praying about the dream, and God gave me two verses, both in *The Message*. At first, He brought to mind Lamentations 3:2:

> *He took me by the hand*
> *And walked me into pitch-black darkness.*

The second passage, Jeremiah 1:11-12, I opened to at random:

> *GOD'S Message came to me:*
> *"What do you see Jeremiah?"*
> *I said, "a walking stick- that's all."*
> *And GOD said, "Good eyes!*
> *I'm sticking with you.*
> *I'll make every word I gave you come true."*

What do you need on a steep, rocky, downhill path? A walking stick, and a companion. Jesus was offering me both! It's also fascinating to me that God not only gave me these passages to confirm the dream, but He also controlled which version of the Bible I grabbed. In the *NIV*, *The New International Version*, the second passage reads like this:

> *The word of the LORD came to me:*
> *"What do you see. Jeremiah?"*
> *"I see the branch of an almond tree," I replied.*
> *The LORD said to me,*
> *"You have seen correctly,*
> *for I am watching to see that my word is*
> *fulfilled."*

And then the translator's note says:

> *The Hebrew for 'watching' sounds like the*
> *Hebrew for 'almond tree.'*

Isn't that cool? God was making a play on words in the Hebrew when he gave the vision to Jeremiah! But in His dealings with *ME,* He knew I needed a walking stick and not an almond branch, so he had me open to that passage in The Message. It was *EXACTLY* what I needed.

A full year passed, and I was now in the hospital with Covid Pneumonia. And God brought this dream to mind. I was in that forest now! The Covid forest. And I was truly frightened. And then, He gave me an attitude check. Early morning on December 26, as I was proning and crying, He brought to mind the waterfall scene from the movie Apocalypto, of all things! He impressed upon me that this was HIS Covid forest. I am His child, and He was walking with me in HIS forest. So I need to not be afraid.

> *He took me by the hand and walked me into*
> *pitch-black darkness.*

Down the hard path into His Covid forest. His territory. And then He led me safely out.

19.   Grab it By the Tail

Often this past year, I have felt "old." And sometimes I would wonder if life had passed me by. If perhaps I had missed God's will, and this life I am currently living was all there was for me. If I am "too old" at age 52 to start over, as my post-covid physical condition may necessitate. But this morning I noticed something interesting. I was reading about the call of Abram, in Genesis 12, quoted from *The Message*:

> GOD told Abram: "Leave your country, your family, and your father's home for a land I will show you..." So Abram left just as GOD said, and Lot was with him. Abram was seventy-five years old...

God totally changed the course of his life at that moment. At age 75. So, it's not too late for me. And it's not too late for you. At age 80, God spoke to Moses for the very first time. It was at the burning bush and described in Exodus 4 and quoted from the NIV:

> So GOD said, "What's that in your hand?"
> "A staff."
> "Throw it to the ground." He threw it. It became a snake; Moses jumped back- fast! GOD said to Moses, "Reach out and grab it by the tail."
>
> [Me as Moses in my best British accent, "RIGHT!!!"]
>
> Moses reached out and grabbed it-- and he was holding his staff again.

Friends, I hate snakes. No, I *LOATHE* them. But sometimes God asks us to do things we find absolutely frightening. To take the snake by the tail. I have been fearful most of my life. This is something God has been dealing with me about lately. *"BE NOT AFRAID!"* So friends, let me encourage you. If you feel that God wants you to do something, then step out. Risk it. No matter your season of life.

Reach out and grab it by the tail.

20. Come and Worship

This morning I opened to Psalm 22-23 in one Bible, noticed it was Psalm 23. Familiar. Okay. Sure. So then I closed it and opened my *OTHER* Bible... to Psalm 22-23. "Righty then!" So I took a closer look and noticed *THESE* verses. Psalm 22:27-31 in *The Message*. I wasn't paying attention the first time, so God brought me there again! Haha!

> *All the power mongers*
> > *are before Him-- worshiping!*
> *All the poor and powerless too—*
> > *Worshiping!*
> *Along with those*
> > *who never got it together-- Worshiping!*

"Those who never got it together..." I feel like that is me some days. (Most days?) Do you feel like you need to get your life together spiritually before you can worship God? Don't worry about it. It's Sunday morning.

Come and worship.

21. Worrying As Usual...

I was complaining to God about work tonight, telling him that it sucked. I was gone all day, spent most of the day driving, and personally accomplished nothing. Our customer is anxious, and NOTHING is going right. But then he showed me Philippians 4:6-7 in *The Message*:

> *Don't fret or worry. Instead of worrying, PRAY.*
> *Let petitions and prayers shape your worries*
> *into prayers, letting God know your concerns.*
> *Before you know it, a sense of God's wholeness,*
> *everything coming together for good, will come*
> *and settle you down. It's wonderful what*
> *happens when Christ displaces worry at the*
> *center of your life.*

Well then!

22. Hiding Place

A few days ago, I was on a long car ride, and the whole time, the song *You Are My Hiding Place* was playing in my head. Those familiar with the song will know it can be sung as a Round, with new voices joining in at different points. The song never really ends. That's fitting, I think.

> *You are my Hiding Place*
> *You always fill my heart*
> *With songs of deliverance*
> *Whenever I am afraid*
> *I will trust in you*

I will trust in you
Let the weak say I am strong,
In the strength of my Lord
I will trust in You.[9]

While this song was playing in my head, God showed me a vision. I was in a cave system on a rocky shoreline. A massive winter storm was raging against the shore where I was at. Waves were surging in and out of the caves, and I had to use the flashes of lightning through gaps overhead to keep from getting soaked. It was frightening. But then I realized I was sheltered in the caves. Had I been on the surface, on the outside, I would have been exposed to not only surf, but to rain and cold and 50 mph winds. Here, I was sheltered.

Sometimes we are battered by storms, and we don't even realize that even at that moment of trial and fury, God is in fact, sheltering us. Sheltering us just as he did with Moses, hiding him in the cleft of the rock, (Exodus 33) while His glory passed by. In my life, the Covid storm battered me, and then Jesus calmed that storm. But God was reminding me that while fresh storms are imminent, I am sheltered in the cleft of the rock.

Whenever I am afraid I will trust in you.

---

[9] Carol Cymbala, Selah, *You Are My Hiding Place*, album Hiding Place, 2004, track 7, produced by Morten Schjolin, Allan Hall, Todd Smith, Nicol Sponberg, and Jason Kyle, Curb Records, Nashville TN. https://www.youtube.com/watch?v=iukRJ9Wnr6A

23. For the Grieving

Some of us are hurting tonight. Some of your griefs I am aware of, and you are on my heart. But this post may find others of you that I don't know well, or I haven't kept up with enough to know your story, but this song came to mind, and I wanted to share it with you. Many times, we as Christians seem to think that we should have a pain-free life. Like perhaps suffering or pain must be God punishing us for our sin. And maybe *if we were spiritual enough*, maybe we wouldn't be hurting so much? But Scripture doesn't teach that. In Isaiah 53, *The Message* tells us about God's son, the Messiah Jesus:

> *Still, it's what GOD had in mind all along, to*
> *crush him with pain.*

Over and over again, Jesus told his followers that he was going to Jerusalem where He must suffer and die, and later be raised to life. If suffering was such a key element of Jesus' life, why do I think I will have it easy? Some of us have sick children, have lost spouses or parents recently, or expect to lose them soon. Others are watching their carefully laid plans and dreams of many years burn up. And the glowing sparks and ashes are flying around you even now. But... God is here, and He sees.

I really love this song, born in pain. I didn't write it, but it moves me. Sometimes God gives songs, and often, the best ones come in times of sorrow. Much like this song *Miracles,* written Chris Quilala after the loss of his stillborn son.

> *The one who made the blind to see*
> *Is moving here in front of me*
> *Moving here in front of me*

The one who made the deaf to hear
Is silencing my every fear
Silencing my every fear

I believe in You, I believe in You
You're the God of Miracles

The one who does impossible
Is reaching out to make me whole
Reaching out to make me whole
The one who put death in its place
His life is flowing through my veins
His life is flowing through my veins!

I believe in You, I believe in You
You're the God of Miracles

The God who was and is to come
The power of the Risen One
The God who brings the dead to life
You're the God of miracles
You're the God of miracles

I believe in You, I believe in You
You're the God of Miracles[10]

---

[10] Chris Quilala, Jesus Culture, *Miracles,* album Let It Echo 2016, produced by Jeremy Edwardson, Sparrow Records, Brentwood TN, https://www.youtube.com/watch?v=S-auXYdMSGM

24. The Desert

I opened at random to this passage three times today (so far?) so maybe I should share it! It is Jeremiah 29:13-14, quoted from *The Message*:

> *When you come looking for me,*
> > *you'll find me.*
> *Yes, when you get serious about finding me*
> > *and want it more than anything else,*
> *I'll make sure you won't be disappointed.*
> > *GOD'S Decree.*

Further on, in Jeremiah 31: 2-3:

> *They found grace out in the desert,*
> > *these people who survived the killing.*
> *Israel, out looking for a place to rest,*
> > *met God out looking for them!"*
> *GOD told them, "I've never quit loving you and*
> *never will.*
> > *Expect love, love, and more love!*

Friends, we usually think of the desert as a place of pain. As a kind of punishment. A lonely place. But... that's not what the desert is for. It's for intimacy. Hosea 2:14-15 in the *NIV* reads:

> *Therefore I am now going to allure her;*
> > *I will lead her into the desert and speak*
> *tenderly to her.*
> *There I will give her back her vineyards,*
> > *and will make the Valley of Achor*
> *[trouble] a door of Hope.*

Has God led you into the desert? Embrace it. It's a privilege, not a punishment. May your desert bloom as you diligently seek Him!

25. The Big Picture

Sometimes we are so focused on our own story that we are blind to what God is really doing. In Exodus 5 (quoted from *The Message*), Moses has been sent to Pharaoh with the message from God, "Let my people go!" But instead, Pharaoh makes it *HARDER*, demanding the same quota, but no longer providing straw for the brickmaking. An angry crowd confronts Moses, and then he goes bellyaching to God.

> *Moses went back to GOD and said, "My Master, why are you treating this people so badly? And why did you ever send me? From the moment I came to Pharaoh to speak in your name, things have only gotten WORSE for this people! And rescue?*
>
> [stomps foot for emphasis]
>
> *Does this look like rescue to you???"*
> *GOD said to Moses, "Now you'll see what I'll do to Pharaoh..."*

This was before the plagues, but Moses didn't know that. *All he could see was the current crisis.*

Some time ago, God showed me my journal. The pages were flipping, as though from the wind, and I was surprised to see blank paragraphs, and even whole blank pages! See, my journal is part diary, part letter to God. I write to Him about my day, my frequent sins, and about what I am stressed about or hurting over. About what's going on in my life. I copy verses that strike me and ask God question after question. I am *VERY* thorough.

And yet, I was seeing paragraphs and whole pages missing! How can that be? But what I think God was telling me was that I didn't know the whole story. Those blank paragraphs and pages represent things God was doing behind my back, and that I was unaware of. Someday, perhaps, He will "fill in the blanks" for me. But for now, I am required to *TRUST* Him. That He *IS* working.

Even when I can't see it.

26. Peculiarly Answered Prayer

Sometimes God answers our prayers, just not in the way we anticipate. In Romans chapter 15, Paul is writing to his friends in Rome about his plans to come visit them soon:

> *I have one request, dear friends: Pray for me.*
> *Pray strenuously with and for me-- to God the*
> *Father, through the power of our Master Jesus*
> *through the love of the Spirit-- that I will be*
> *delivered from the lion's den of unbelievers in*
> *Judea. Pray also that my relief offering to the*
> *Jerusalem Christians be accepted in the spirit*
> *in which it is given. Then, God willing, I'll be*
> *on my way to you with a light and eager heart,*
> *looking forward to being refreshed by your*

company. God's peace be with all of you. Oh,
yes!

Romans 15:30-33 The Message

Years ago, the Azerbaijan Bible Society went to great effort and expense to have a number of Bibles printed in Azeri and shipped into the country. As part of the legal requirements for the organization, they were required to be *very* inclusive in their membership. One of these members, a former KGB type, procured the warehouse where the Bibles were stored. Due to political intrigue, he fell under suspicion and the warehouse was raided. By the time the Bible Society arrived, the warehouse was empty. Totally cleaned out. All the precious Bibles were gone! Utter disaster. But then they noticed a strange thing. All around the capital and in other major cities, every sidewalk book seller had Bibles for sale! And they all sold.

Paul had been praying to visit his friends in Rome, and God arranged it, albeit as a prisoner. The Bible Society had been praying that God would distribute the Bibles, and God arranged that too!

May we each recognize and embrace God's presence and movement, even when it looks different from what we were expecting!

27. In the Waiting Room

Do you ever feel like God has you waiting? This seems like a theme in my walk with God lately. Some time ago, I was asking God about something, and in response He showed me a waiting room. And not an especially nice one either. A 1970's doctor's office (think Naval Hospital), with linoleum floors, bad lighting, dingy walls, and metal chairs with torn vinyl seats. The seats were red, and the wait time was indeterminate. Ugh.

There is a picture going around Instagram that I really love, of a new mother holding her newborn, with a look of such joy and surprise on her face. It was to be her first baby, and she spent most of her pregnancy planning the perfect hospital birth experience. Everything was arranged. But Covid complications at the hospital end made it all fall apart, and she ended up having her baby at home – after 18 hours of labor. But she did it!

Paul uses this pregnant waiting as a spiritual analogy in Romans 8: 18-28. Here it is, quoted from The Message:

> *That's why I don't think there is any comparison between the present hard times and the coming good times. The created world itself can hardly wait for what's coming next. Everything in creation is being more or less held back. God reins it in until both creation and all the creatures are ready and can be released at the same moment into the glorious times ahead. Meanwhile, the joyful anticipation deepens.*
>
> *All around us we observe a pregnant creation. The difficult times of pain throughout the world are simply birth pangs. But it's not only around us; it's within us. The Spirit of God is arousing us within. We're also feeling the birth pangs. These sterile and barren bodies of ours are yearning for full deliverance. That is why*

*waiting does not diminish us, any more than
waiting diminishes a pregnant mother. We are
enlarged in the waiting. We, of course, don't
see what is enlarging us. But the longer we
wait, the larger we become, [Ha!] and the
more joyful our expectancy.*

*Meanwhile, the moment we get tired in the
waiting, God's Spirit is right alongside, helping
us along. If we don't know how or what to pray,
it doesn't matter. He does our praying in and
for us, making prayer out of our wordless
sighs, our aching groans. He knows us far
better than we know ourselves, knows our
pregnant condition, and keeps us present
before God. That's why we can be so sure that
every detail in our lives of love for God is
worked into something good.*

Sometimes, I think God deliberately makes us wait, to get us to
seek Him harder. A beautiful example is found in Song of Songs
5: 2-6, quoted from *The Message*:

*I was sound asleep,
        but in my dreams I was wide awake.
Oh, listen!
        It's the sound of my lover knocking,
calling!*

*"Let me in, dear companion, dearest friend,
        my dove, consummate lover!
I'm soaked with the dampness of the night,
        drenched with dew, shivering and cold."*

49

"But I'm in my nightgown—
do you expect me to get dressed?
I'm bathed and in bed-
do you want me to get dirty?"

But my lover wouldn't take no for an answer,
and the longer he knocked, the more
excited I became.

I got up to open the door to my lover,
sweetly ready to receive him,
desiring and expectant
as I turned the door handle.
But when I opened the door he was gone.
My loved one had tired of waiting and
left.

So, are you waiting? Are you tired of waiting? (Uh-huh.) Press in.

Wait a bit longer.

28. The God-Who-Makes-Things-Happen

Psalm 77:14 in the NIV, *The New International Version* says:

You are the God who performs miracles;
you display your power among the
peoples.

That's true. But I prefer how *The Message* phrases it:

You're the God who makes things happen;
you showed everyone what you can do.

50

I really like that. There are many Hebrew names for God... except I don't speak Hebrew? They are nice to learn about, but this *WORKS* for me.

The - God - Who - Makes - Things - Happen.

I like that. An English language name for God that resonates with me. Here's another:

The - God - Whose - Timing - Is - Perfect.

I needed to keep that aspect of His character in mind, so I wrote a song to remember it. My own timing sucks, but *HIS* timing is perfect. Sometimes we get ahead of God, like Abram and Hagar. Abram was given the promise of a son, but ten years passed. *TEN YEARS* – and nothing. So he and his wife decided to make things happen... which led to the birth of Ishmael and three millennia of warfare.

Years ago, God warned me about Abraham and Hagar. Not to try to make things happen in a situation I was struggling in. And then He showed me little pizzas baking in the oven. In the vision, I opened the door, grabbed the cookie sheet they were on, but was in too much of a hurry. They slid off the cookie sheet and ended up upside down on the heating element on the bottom of the oven. Goo everywhere. Pizzas ruined. So, did I listen to the double warning? Of course not! I made a big mess, and now I am banished from the kitchen.

Because He is **The – God – Who - Makes – Things - Happen.** It's *HIS* job, not mine. And He is also **The – God – Whose – Timing – Is - Perfect.** Are you asking God to make things happen? Keep asking. Is God telling you to wait? Sit your butt down then and *TRUST* Him.

He has a plan.

29.   Love and Toddlers

This morning I was praying about something, and in response, God quoted 1 Corinthians 13:11 out of the *NIV* to me:

> *When I was a child, I talked like a child, I*
> *thought like a child, I reasoned like a child.*
> *When I became a man, I put childish ways*
> *behind me.*

What did this mean for me exactly? Think of a toddler who thinks only of themselves... *THEY* are hungry. *THEY* are thirsty. *THEY* want the blue cup. (Yesterday it was the yellow cup). *THEY* don't want to get in the car seat. Everything is about them. They don't see the big picture, or perhaps they just don't care. And God was calling me childish and telling me to grow up.

Are you familiar with this chapter? It is called The Love Chapter. And it's Valentine's Day. *DING DING DING DING!* Nope. Not subtle. (I don't do subtle. I lack the capacity. God knows this.) There's a reason these verses are in The Love Chapter.

> *Love is PATIENT. Love is kind...*

Love is not childish. Have you ever met a patient toddler?

> *Love never fails...*
>
> *Now we see but a poor reflection as in a*
> *mirror; then we will see face to face. Now I*

*know in part; then I shall know fully, even as I
am fully known...*

You see, I was acting childish, I was thinking only of myself. I was missing the big picture. I didn't have all the facts! And then God reminded me of the vision he gave me awhile back, of the pages flipping in my journal. Paragraphs and even whole pages were blank. Because God was working behind my back-- I just couldn't see it. I didn't know the whole story. But someday, He will fill in all the blanks.

Now I know in part; then I shall know fully...

I don't know the big picture. I can't. But I have to trust that Father God does, and is working for my good, even when I don't understand all the reasons. And the restraint of the car seat that I am fighting so hard against? It's so He can take me on an adventure! So have a little trust already!

Because He's a good Father.

30. Ripped Away

Have you ever been in a place where you felt like you had things reasonably together, your life on track, and then suddenly it was all ripped away and you were thrown into a new and difficult period of your life? Perhaps the death of a spouse or child, the loss of a job, a broken relationship, or a devastating house fire? It seems so... unfair. The Bible is full of such situations. Daniel 1, Esther 2, and Job 1 come immediately to mind. In Daniel 1, quoted from *The Message,* we read:

The Master handed King Jehoiakim of Judah over to [Nebuchadnezzar], along with some of the furnishings from the Temple of God. Nebuchadnezzar took the king and furnishings to the country of Babylon, the ancient Shinar. He put the furnishings in the sacred treasury.

The king told Ashpenaz, head of the palace staff, to get some Israelites from the royal family and nobility-- young men who were healthy and handsome, intelligent and well-educated, good prospects for leadership positions in the government, perfect specimens! -- and indoctrinate them into the Babylonian language and the lore of magic and fortunetelling. The king then ordered that they be served from the same menu as the royal table – the best food, the finest wine. After three years of training they would be given positions in the kings court...

I'm sure Daniel and his friends were not at all pleased to be ripped from their homes, their good schools, and their friends and taken prisoner to Babylon. And their best shot at justice-- petitioning the king for a chance to go home, would not be for another three years. Hurry up and wait... But they had no way of knowing that 11 years later, Nebuchadnezzar would destroy Jerusalem and the temple. Nearly all of the survivors would be either executed or taken prisoner to Babylon. Yet Daniel and his friends were already there, in safety. It was a rescue, in advance. Not only that, but it was also *a Divine Set-Up.* God was setting them up to use them in Babylon. But getting there was a path of pain.

In Esther 2, King Xerxes decrees that *EVERY* beautiful young virgin in the Empire be brought to the palace for his personal use sexually, and the one he liked best would be the next queen.

Before a girl's turn came to go into King Xerxes, she had to complete twelve months of beauty treatments prescribed for women, six months with oil of myrrh and six with perfumes and cosmetics. And this was how she would go to the king: Anything she wanted was given with her from the harem to the kings palace. In the evening she would go there and in the morning return to another part of the harem to the car of Shaashgaz, the king's eunuch who was in charge of the concubines. She would not return to the king unless he was pleased with her and summoned her by name.

When the turn came for Esther... she asked nothing other than what Hegai, the king's eunuch who was in charge of the harem, suggested. And Esther won the favor of everyone who saw her. She was taken to King Xerxes in the royal residence in the tenth month, the month of Tebeth, in the seventh year of his reign.

Now the king was attracted to Esther more than to any of the other women, and she won his favor and approval more than any of the other

virgins. So he set a royal crown on her head
and made her queen instead of Vashti... (NIV).

Okay, she eventually gets to be queen, but think about it from her perspective. She is ripped from her family to become the probable concubine (permanent sex slave) of a king who has countless other women. King Xerxes divorced Queen Vashti halfway into the third year of his reign, but he didn't get around to Esther until the tenth month of the seventh year of his reign. So approximately four years have passed. If you account for the year of beauty treatments, that's over a thousand fresh virgins before it's her turn to get deflowered by the king. (Big deal.) A serious body count, in today's dating terms. And who knows how many women he had before the Parade - of - Virgins. And what about her plans? Was she already engaged to a nice young Jewish boy when she was rudely taken to the palace? Were they daydreaming together about their future together, and how many kids they were going to have? *DIDN'T GOD CARE ABOUT HER DREAMS?* But God already had a plan. She couldn't know it, but it was a *Divine Set-Up.* God was setting her up to save her nation. But I'll bet she cried her heart out along the way.

Job lost his riches, his children, and his health, all at once. His wife urged him to curse God and die. But his response in Job 1:21 *(NIV)* was:

> *The Lord gave, and the Lord has taken away;*
> *may the name of the LORD be praised.*

Years ago, I was praying hard about a situation, and begging God to intervene. In response, I felt the urge to open Instagram. The very first image to come up was a bracelet inscribed with

Psalm 46:10. *"Be still and know that I am God."* God was telling me to cool it. That He was in control. Yes, God.

So friends, maybe your life is an unexpected disaster. A path of pain. And as is often the case, there is no answer coming to your question of "WHY???" But maybe God is setting you up for something? I pray you receive grace for your journey with Him in this time of pain.

And may joy come in the morning.

31.   Troubled Hearts

Yesterday I was watching YouTube videos about the war in Ukraine, and about the cascading flow of events. Putin threatening nuclear war. China crouching in readiness to spring onto Taiwan. NATO mobilizing the rapid response force for the first time ever... Grim stuff for sure.

Then the song *You Are My Hiding Place* started playing in my head:

> *You are my hiding place*
> *You always fill my heart*
> *With songs of deliverance*
> *Whenever I am afraid*
> *I will trust in you* [11]

---

[11] Carol Cymbala, Selah, *You Are My Hiding Place,* album Hiding Place, 2004, track 7, produced by Morten Schjolin, Allan Hall, Todd Smith, Nicol Sponberg, and Jason Kyle, Curb Records, Nashville TN.
https://www.youtube.com/watch?v=iukRJ9Wnr6A

And then I thought back to the vision God gave me of being in a cluster of caves on a rocky shoreline, while a massive winter storm pounded the outside, and water surged in and out. It was frightening, to be sure. But I was sheltered.

While I was thinking about this, God spoke John 14:1 *(NIV)* to me.

> *Do not let your hearts be troubled.*
> *Trust in God; trust also in me.*

Were the listeners' hearts troubled? You betcha. The scene was the last supper. Jesus had been telling his disciples all along that he would be betrayed and killed. And he had just told them that it was finally time for his betrayal, and that he was about to die. Peter protested and got told he would deny Jesus that very night. Three times. So yeah, I would say their hearts were troubled.

> *Let not your hearts be troubled,*
> *neither let them be afraid.*

A great Storm is already battering believers in Ukraine, and I believe it will reach our shoreline soon. My prayer is that God will give us grace and courage, and that we will not deny Him.

> *You are my hiding place;*
> *you will protect me from trouble*
> *and surround me*
> *with songs of deliverance.*
> *-Psalm 32:7 (NIV)*

32. What Are You Afraid Of?

I, I'm the One comforting you.
*   What are you afraid of, or who?*
Some man or woman
*   who will soon be dead?*
Some poor wretch
*   destined for dust?*

You've forgotten me, GOD,
*   who made you,*
who unfurled the skies,
*   who founded the earth.*

And here you are, quaking like an aspen before
the tantrums
*   of a tyrant who thinks he can kick down*
the world.

*   -Isaiah 51:12-13 The Message*

33. Is ANYTHING too hard for me?

In Jeremiah 32, Judah was at war. Nebuchadnezzar, king of Babylon had been besieging it since the previous year, and things were looking really bad. Moreover, God's prophet Jeremiah was a prisoner, for prophesying the fall of Jerusalem to the Babylonians. *"Not Helpful"*, as we might say. And then God told Jeremiah to do something strange. He told Jeremiah that his cousin was going to ask him to buy his field. Sure enough, it happened just as God said.

I knew that this was the word of the LORD; so I
bought the field at Anathoth from my
cousin Hanamel and weighed out for him
seventeen shekels of silver on the scales. I took
the deed of purchas – the sealed copy
containing the terms and conditions as well as
the unsealed copy – and I gave this deed to
Baruch son of Neriah, the son of Maheilah, in
the presence of my cousin Hanamel and of the
witnesses who had signed the deed and of all
the Jews sitting in the courtyard of the guard.

In their presence I gave Baruch these
instructions: This is what the LORD Almighty,
the God of Israel says: "Take these documents,
both the sealed and unsealed copies of the deed
of purchase and put them in a clay jar so that
they will last a long time. For this is what the
LORD Almighty, the God of Israel, says:
Houses, fields and vineyards will again be
bought in this land." After I had given the deed
of purchase to Baruch son of Neriah, I prayed
to the LORD:

"Ah, Sovereign LORD, you have made the
heavens and the earth by your outstretched
arm. Nothing is too hard for you..."

"See how the siege ramps are built up to take
the city. Because of the sword, famine and
plague, the city WILL be handed over to the
Babylonians who are attacking it. What you
said has happened, as you now see. And though

the city will be handed over to the Babylonians,
you, O Sovereign LORD, say to me 'Buy the
field with silver, and have the transaction
witnessed' " (NIV.)

Friends, have you ever questioned God? Has God ever told you to do something that makes no sense whatsoever? Is ludicrous, even? Here Jeremiah is a royal *PRISONER*. Worse yet, the city is about to fall. They're probably all going to die. And God is telling him to buy a field, pay silver, have it witnessed, record the documents in the usual manner, when it is all about to be destroyed??? This is the *END*. And yet God tells him to buy a field that he can't even go look at, much less make a profit from farming it. Waste of time and money. You're kidding, right?

Then the word of the LORD came to Jeremiah:
"I am the LORD, the God of all mankind. Is
anything too hard for me?

Therefore, this is what the LORD says: I am
about to hand this city over to the Babylonians
and to Nebuchadnezzar king of Babylon, who
will capture it. The Babylonians who
are attacking the city will come in and set it on
fire; they will burn it down..."

"You are saying about this city, 'By the sword,
famine and plague it will be handed over to the
king of Babylon'; but this is what the LORD,
the God of Israel says: I will surely gather them
from all the lands where I banish them in my
furious anger and wrath; I will bring them back
to this place and let them live in safety.

They will be my people, and I will be their
God..."

God was trying to make a point. To use Jeremiah as a living sermon illustration. (Lucky him.) God was telling them that although it looked like the end, it really wasn't.

> *This is what the LORD says: As I have brought*
> *all this great calamity on this people, so I will*
> *give them all the prosperity I have promised*
> *them. Once more, fields will be bought in this*
> *land of which you say, 'It is a desolate waste,*
> *without men or animals, for it has been handed*
> *over to the Babylonians.' Fields will be bought*
> *for silver, and the deeds signed, sealed and*
> *witnessed in the territory of Benjamin, in the*
> *villages around Jerusalem, in the towns of*
> *Judah and in the towns of the hill country, of*
> *the western foothills and the Negev, because I*
> *will restore their fortunes, declares the LORD."*

Friends, I believe hard times are ahead. For Ukraine, they are here now. And I believe Poland and the Baltics will be next, which will bring us into the war. Putin has threatened to use nukes, and it may come to that, but God is still present. And he is big enough and GOD enough to be with us, no matter the size of the trouble or heartache. So we are not to be fearful.

> *I am the LORD, the God of all mankind. Is*
> *anything too hard for me?*
>
> *-Jeremiah 32:27*

Matthew 14:27 *(MSG)* and other passages tell us about a frightening storm at sea. But Jesus was there, walking on the water.

Courage. It's me. Don't be afraid.

For some of us, the storm is coming. For others, you're already in it. The siege ramps are built, and the mighty battering ram is positioned at the gate. Yet Jesus says, "Take courage. It's me. Don't be afraid."

"I will not fear though tens of thousands draw up against me on every side..."
-Psalm 3:6 (NIV)

34. Behind the Scenes

Job 9:10-11 in *The Message* caught my eye this morning:

*We'll never comprehend
        all the great things he does;
his miracle surprises
        can't be counted.*

*Somehow, though he moves right in front of me,
        I don't see him;
quietly but surely he's active,
        and I miss it.*

I really love that last line. "Quietly but surely he's active, and I miss it!" That's so true. God *IS* working behind the scenes. Sometimes he is ahead of us, like a worker walling off a door with drywall that he doesn't want us to try to go through, so by the time we arrive, we have no knowledge a door was ever there. At other times, he unlocks a door, and it springs open before we even raise a fist to knock.

The song *Way Maker* has some really great lyrics:

> *Even when I don't see it,*
> *You're working.*
> *Even when I don't feel it,*
> *You're working.*
> *You never stop,*
> *You never stop working.* [12]

It's true though. God IS working behind the scenes. I ask that He open our eyes a little today. To let us get a peek behind the scenes, at the awesome things He is doing!

35. Lice Eggs

Some time ago I was stressing over some details. Things I was worried about. I was practically hyperventilating in my prayer time. "But God, what about this?!?! And God, THIS thing has to happen! And what about THAT???"

In response, God showed me something strange. He showed me His own hand holding a test tube full of nits. Little white lice eggs. They represented all the little details I was stressing over-- plus the ones I hadn't even known to look for. He impressed

---

[12] Osinachi Okoro, Leeland, *Way Maker,* Better Word, 2019, track3, Integrity Music, Brentwood TN, https://www.youtube.com/watch?v=iJCV_2H9xD0

upon me that this was *ALL* of them. I had been nit-picking – stressing over all the little details – when He had already got them *all*. The test tube was firmly sealed with a stopper, it was held tightly in His hand, and He wasn't going to let go.

So no, I don't know all the details. But *HE* does. My job is to trust him and enjoy the ride.

36. The Day God ACTED

I opened this morning to Psalm 118:23-24. *The New International Version* phrases it:

> *The LORD has done this,*
> *and it is marvelous in our eyes.*
> *This is the day the LORD has made;*
> *let us rejoice and be glad in it.*

Three of the gospels record Jesus quoting this verse and applying it to himself, and God has been using it to speak to me about things He is doing. As such, it has been a great comfort to me. But this morning, I noticed something new. *The Message* has a different take:

> *This is GOD's work.*
> *We rub our eyes – we can hardly*
> *believe it!*
> *This very day GOD acted—*
> *let's celebrate and be festive!*

I had always taken verse 22 ("this is the day the LORD has made") in a very general Hallmark Moment kind of way.

Wake up sleepy head! It's a beautiful day!
Birds and Butterflies! Time to get stuff done.
Yesterday SUCKED, but today is a Brand-New
Day!

(Clearly I am way over-caffeinated.)

But no, this is not a general-purpose feel-good-moment. This is a *SPECIFIC* moment.

This is the very day God ACTED—
let's celebrate and be festive!

Do you need God to *ACT* in your life? To intervene? I sure do! Isaiah 64:4 reads in the *NIV*:

Since ancient times, no one has heard, no ear
has perceived, no eye has seen
any God besides you, who ACTS on behalf of
those who wait for him.

So, God *DOES* act. And waiting patiently (or otherwise?) seems to be part of it. In Acts 13:2, they were fasting and waiting for guidance, when God spoke and told them to set apart Paul and Barnabas for their new assignment.

So, have you been asking God to Act, but you are still waiting? It turns out waiting is pretty normal. So, wait then. Wait in earnest expectation of God's action.

And keep asking!

37. Rhetorical Questions

I woke up with this Chris Tomlin song *Is He Worthy* on my heart and wanted to share it with you. This a "Call and Response" style song, full of rhetorical questions.

> *Do you feel the world is broken? (We do)*
> *Do you feel the shadows deepen? (We do)*
> *But do you know that all the dark*
> *won't keep the light from getting through? (We do)*
> *And do you wish that you could see it all made new? (We do)...*

The shadows ARE deepening, but He *IS* Worthy.

> *Does the Father truly love us? (He does)*
> *And does the Spirit move among us? (He does.)*
> *And does Jesus our Messiah hold forever those he loves? (He does)*
> *And does God intend to dwell again with us? (He does)* [13]

God seems to relish using rhetorical questions to remind us of truths that should be obvious. In Jeremiah 32, God tells Jeremiah to buy a field, pay silver, and have it duly recorded. Jeremiah points out that the city is about to be conquered by the Babylonians, "So why bother?" God answers him with a rhetorical question in verse 27:

---

[13] Andrew Peterson, Ben Shive, Chris Tomlin, *Is He Worthy,* album Holy Roar, 2018, track 8, produced by Ed Cash, Sparrow Records, Brentwood TN, https://www.youtube.com/watch?v=FkRiYsTN7KY

*I am the God of all mankind. Is anything too
hard for me?"*

So, is God asking us rhetorical questions? Are we paying attention?

*I am the God of all mankind. Is ANYTHING too
hard for me?*

No, Lord...

38.   A Fresh Start

*Clean the slate God, so we can
        start the day fresh!
Keep me from stupid sins,
        From thinking I can take over your
work.*
                        Psalm 19:13, The Message

Enough said!

39.   Homecoming

"Christ is RISEN!" was the Call, and the Easter greeting on the mouth of the Soviet believers. And the Response, the 2nd half of the password was "He is Risen INDEED!"

The song *Rattle!* starts out with these lyrics:

*Saturday was silent— Surely it was through!
Since when has impossible ever stopped you?*

*Friday's disappointment is Sunday's empty
tomb!
Since when has impossible ever stopped You?
This is the sound of dry bones rattlin'...[14]*

As a young man in the mid 90's, I was privileged to spend time in Azerbaijan, one of the former Soviet Socialist Republics. The population is nearly entirely Shia Muslim, the language is in the Turkic language family, and the culture is Persian. Azerbaijan is in the Caucasus mountains region, and is bordered by Russia, Georgia, Armenia, Turkey, Iran, and the Caspian Sea. And I *LOVE* the place...

I was part of a small local church there in the capital. We met in the Puppet Theater on Wednesday nights, and in a different theater on Sunday mornings. Snow outside in the winter, and no heat, as I recall. Your heavy winter outside clothes were also your Sunday morning go-to-church clothes. Convenient! The church had been started by a Finnish missionary during communism, and preaching was in English, with translation into Russian and Azeri. The pastor spoke excellent Russian, but this arrangement helped the local believers who were learning English as well as the odd expat (ME!) who severely lacked language skills...

Eventually, I had to return to the US, but had the unexpected opportunity to return in 2003 and 2004 on business trips. And so on Easter Sunday 2003, I found myself back at my old church in Baku. Much had changed. The church was HUGE now, with

---

[14] Brandon Lake, Chris Brown, Steve Furtick, *RATTLE! (Morning and Evening),* album Graves Into Gardens, 2020, track 1, Elevation Worship Records, Matthews NC, https://www.youtube.com/watch?v=xrAdbH28gIg

hundreds of people! My old friends were married now and speaking Azeri to each other instead of Russian. My Azeri friend who had done the translating was now the pastor. This time, the preaching was in Azeri, with translation into Russian and English. A woman sang a solo in Azeri about the Resurrection. I couldn't understand the words, but the haunting beauty of the song broke me. I wept and wept. My friends asked me how things had changed. My reply, in my horrible broken Russian was:

> *For these past seven years, my heart was a*
> *foreigner, but now I am at home.*

And that's how it felt that Easter Sunday nineteen years ago. That I had come home. But for believers, home isn't a place. It's a Person. The Lord Jesus Christ. And I am looking forward to that homecoming...

> *Souls tend*
> *To go back*
> *To who feels*
> *Like home.*
> *-N.R. Hart*

Christ is Risen!!!

40. WAIT

May I share something cool God did today?

This morning I was stressing about something. (I wasn't talking to God about it, mind you. I was just turning it over and over in my mind, like a Rubik's Cube I was trying to solve.) My wife's BFF, Sharon Cohn Wu, can solve these things blindfolded. I can't solve one with my eyes open and unlimited time. I just can't. I know this... But yet my little two-cylinder mind was still hopelessly banging away at the problem, with smoke coming out of my ears.

But at that very moment God interrupted my thoughts (how rude!) by showing me a meme of Psalm 27:14, which my friend Amanda Hughes had shared earlier this week.

> *Wait for the LORD;*
> *be strong and take heart*
> *and WAIT for the LORD.*

I had completely forgotten about it, but there it was in front of my eyes. As I read, it became like a scene from Alice in Wonderland. The word "Wait" in the bottom left corner of the meme began to grow. As it grew, the font gradually changed to the most beautiful cursive writing-- better than in any illuminated manuscript. It grew until it filled half my vision.

What God was telling me, was to *WAIT*. To do nothing. This is not my puzzle to figure out. It's literally not my problem. It's *GOD's* problem. I didn't need to devote any more thought to it. And the fact that it was in gorgeous cursive? That was because waiting on God in trust and expectation-- is a *beautiful* thing.

He's in The Waiting.

41.　He Loves Me!

I opened to this passage at random last night, and again just now. I think it just might be my favorite scripture passage, and I wanted to share it. It is from Jeremiah 31:1-2, in *The Message*:

> *This is the way GOD put it:*
>
> *They found grace out in the desert,*
> *　　these people who survived the killing.*
> *Israel, out looking for a place to rest*
> *　　met God out looking for them!"*
> *GOD told them, "I've never quit loving you and*
> *never will.*
> *　　Expect love, love, and more love!*

Some of us may be asking right now, "Does God actually love me?" And God's answer, right here in this passage, is an emphatic *YES!!!*

He loves me!

42.　When WE name GOD

Names are important. Names in the Bible often give insight into character. Sometimes God reveals his character by telling us one of his names. But *SOMETIMES*... sometimes we create our *own* names for God as we encounter Him.

In Genesis 16, Hagar was in serious trouble. Her childless boss Sarah had arranged Hagar's marriage to her own elderly husband as a 2nd wife, specifically to get her pregnant. (Oh joy.) She gets pregnant, first wife becomes abusive, and so Hagar runs away. She stops to rest at a stream – exhausted, destitute, quite pregnant, and out of options. In this moment of crisis, God appears to her, and tells the runaway to go back home to her difficult marriage. Moreover, God also tells her the name of her unborn child, his incredible future, and of his character.

In response, Hagar names God **"El Roi"**, The **Strong - God - Who - Sees - Me.** Sometimes we wonder if God sees us. If he sees the trouble we're in-- and if He even cares? In the movie *Avatar*, the most meaningful greeting is *"I SEE you."* As in, "I see into you. I see what you're all about, and I *still* choose to be here." Hagar felt that love, that acceptance, and her heart's response was *"You are The - God - Who - Sees - Me."* Put another way, *"You are The - God- Who - Loves - Me - As - I - Am."* Wow. Powerful stuff!

In Exodus 3:13-14, God has just told Moses at the burning bush to go tell the Hebrews that the God of their fathers had sent him. So Moses asks what name to tell them. But instead of giving a proper name, God gives a descriptive name:

> *"I - AM - WHO - I - AM. Tell them I AM has sent you."*

God was proclaiming his eternal character. Millenia later, Jesus asserts his identity *AND* his character in John 8:56. He is having a discussion with people who were relying on their ancestry as children of Abraham as proof of their identity and character, and Jesus told them "Your father Abraham rejoiced to see my day, and he saw it and was glad." They were incredulous. *"You are not yet 50 years old, and you have seen Abraham?"* (You're kidding, right?) Jesus then countered their argument by proclaiming his OWN identity and character by saying simply, *"Before Abraham was, I AM."* He was saying that he was **THE** Great I AM who appeared to Moses at the burning bush. And he was combining present tense and past tense to show that he is *TIMELESS.* He is beyond Time. He is self-existent. And so we can trust our times, our timelines, our Eternity – in his hands.

I really love these long, hyphenated character names. I think they're cool. In Psalm 23, David comes up with one: **The - Lord - Who - Shepherds - Me**. One I use regularly is **The - God - Whose - Timing - Is - Perfect**. My current favorite is found in Joel 2:26, in *The Message.*

> *You'll eat your fill of good food.*
> *You'll be full of praise to your GOD,*
> ***The - God - Who - Has - Set - You - Back - On***
> ***- Your - Heels - In - Wonder.***

Has God ever set you back on your heels in wonder? How about write about it? Facebook is a good place to start. Maybe somebody needs to hear what God is doing in your life. So go for it. Spit it out. Be bold!

May **The – God – Who – Has – Set – You – Back – On – Your – Heels – In - Wonder** be with you!

43. Broken Lego Dreams

"GOD made my life complete
when I placed all the pieces before him.
When I got my act together,
he gave me a fresh start.
Now I'm alert to GOD's ways:
I don't take God for granted.
Every day I review the way he works,
I try not to miss a trick.
I feel put back together,
and I'm watching my step.
God rewrote the text of my life
when I opened the book of my heart to
his eyes."
                    - Psalm 18:20-24, The Message

Yesterday, I was minding my own business, thinking about stuff, and God spoke to me:

Everything put together.

Okay, sure. I wrote it down, and promptly forgot about it until last night, when I opened to Psalm 41:12 in *The Message:*

You know me inside and out,
you hold me together...

Then this morning in my quiet time, Amy Grant's song *Breath of Heaven* started playing in my head:

Breath of heaven
Hold me together
Be forever near me
Breath of heaven

While that song was still in my head, I opened to Psalm 18 in *The Message:*

> *GOD made my life complete*
>> *when I placed all the pieces before him...*
>
> ...
>
> *I feel put back together*
>> *and I'm watching my step.*

I'm a little slow, but I'm sensing a theme here? Friends, do you feel like you're unraveling? Like some days, you're barely holding it together? That you're trying to carry too many things, you only have so many hands, and you're starting to drop stuff?

Same.

> *God made my life complete*
>> *when I placed all the pieces before him.*

Sometimes, things *need* to fall apart. Things we have created ourselves that God wants to go away because he has something *better* planned.

Some time ago, I was praying and saw a Lego creation, falling as though from a high shelf. It shattered on the floor, into a thousand pieces. "What is this God?" I asked. *"Broken Lego Dreams"* was His reply. And as I watched, a big Zamboni ice machine came into view, swept all those broken pieces away, and smoothed the ice so the game could begin.

So friends, I don't know if you need God to hold you together, or to sweep your Broken Lego Dreams aside and prepare you for the start of the next game-- but God does. So place all your pieces before him, broken or otherwise, and ask Him to move.

He's really good with broken pieces.

44.   Monsters in the Darkness

When I was a child I lived in some houses with basements. The stairs to the basements were always simple affairs, just joists and tread, no risers. So one could *theoretically* get trapped. Even worse was the light setup. There was invariably a single light switch at the top of the stairs. There were several times when I went down to the basement to look for something, and my mother would see that the door was open and the light was on. She would turn the light off, in annoyance at the careless child who accidentally left it on and was wasting electricity. And then she would shut the door...

And then there was darkness. And, presumably, monsters.

I was afraid of the dark. I still am. Because I like seeing what else is there. I like advance notice of what might hurt me. It's one of the reasons I don't like swimming in lakes or the ocean, because I want to be able to see what is in the water with me. I have this delusion that if I could *SEE* the shark swimming under me, that I could then protect myself. Ha!

We readily equate darkness with evil, and that is a good analogy. But we also equate darkness with the unknown. In I Kings 8, King Solomon had just completed building a magnificent temple, and was presiding at the dedication ceremony. *The Message* paraphrase tells us:

> *Then Solomon spoke:*
>
> *GOD has told us that he lives in the dark,*
>   *where no one can see him.*

The New International Version words it as,

> *The LORD has said that he*
> *Would dwell in a dark cloud.*

So here we sometimes find ourselves in our private darkness, frightened by what we can't see-- frightened by what we don't know. Frightened by our lack of control. And yet, the above passage tells us that God *lives* in darkness. And He is here, with us, ***in our darkness***. In our unknown.

Years ago, I was in crisis. I needed to make decisions about the future, and there were too many unknowns. I was panicking and was crying out to God. And then He gave me a startling vision in response to my desperate prayer. In the vision, I was swimming in the middle of the ocean, at midnight, in utter darkness. But there was a spotlight right on me. I could see about two feet in any direction. Just far enough not to bump my head against an obstacle, but no farther. I was demanding details from God, but He was telling me to just keep swimming. He would keep me out of trouble. My job was not to stress about what toothy creatures were swimming alongside me, or how far from shore I was, or where the nearest boat was. It was to just keep swimming. Jesus told his disciples in Matthew 16:24, quoted from *The Message:*

> *Anyone who intends to come with me has to let*
> *me lead.*
> *You're not in the driver's seat; I am.*

And sometimes where he leads us... is into darkness. A place where we don't understand. Where we can't see. Where we are not in control. Jeremiah testified in Lamentations 3:2, quoted from *The Message,*

He took me by the hand and walked me into
pitch-black darkness...

But yet, He *DWELLS* in darkness-- in our darkness with us as believers. And since He is **WITH US** in our darkness, in our unknown, we don't need to be afraid.

45. Let ME be the Daddy

When my children were younger, one of them would regularly try to "parent" their older sibling, correcting their behavior around the house. Predictably, it wasn't going well. I had to pull them aside and tell them "Let ME be the daddy." We chuckle, but it was a real problem. Yet we do the same with God! Years ago, I was pleading with God about a situation, telling him all the reasons why I was upset, and begging Him to intervene. But instead of answering, he led me to open Instagram, and I was staring at this bracelet.

Be still and know that I am God.
                    - Psalm 46:10 (NIV)

God was essentially telling me to quit squawkin' and let HIM be the Daddy! Hillary Scott addresses this in the song *Thy Will*, and the lyrics read:

Sometimes I gotta STOP
Remember that you're God

And I am not![15]

Ecclesiastes 3 tells us there is a time for everything. It's a long litany of contrasts: Birth and death, planting and uprooting, killing and healing, tearing down and building up, weeping and laughing, mourning and dancing, and the list goes on...

But I would add one to this list: *"A time to press in, laboring in prayer, and a time to say "Yes, God," and yield to God's "No."* In my own situation, God made it clear to me it was time to yield to his sovereignty, but He is not always so direct.

I pray that each of us will be able to discern for ourselves when to labor in prayer, and when to discern a "no" and move on. So are you wondering that for yourself, whether to keep asking, or to let God be God? Well, ask Him! (His answer may surprise you.)

Then do whatever He tells you.

46.   Waiting for Answers

I've been noodling on something this morning: the waiting for answers. Sometimes (almost always?) God makes us wait for the fulfillment of his promises, but often God is silent for a season, making us wait for the answers themselves.

In Hosea 1, as an object lesson, God tells his prophet to marry a promiscuous woman and have children by her. He obeys. She

---

[15] Bernie Herms, Emily Lynn Weisband, Hillary Scott, *Thy Will,* album Love Remains, 2016, track 7, produced by Ricky Scaggs, EMI, Nashville TN, https://www.youtube.com/watch?v=Dp4WC_YZAuw

gets pregnant (kids happen), and they have a son. Then God speaks again, naming the child. But here's the thing. Hosea was obedient, but I'm sure he had questions for God. I'll bet he had questions for God every single day of his wife's pregnancy. But there were no answers until the baby came. But still, he waited. And patiently lived his life during The Waiting.

In John 20, the disciples (except Thomas) had seen the risen Christ. We like to say, "seeing is believing." But Thomas went a step further, declaring that he wouldn't believe unless he can *TOUCH* the nail holes. It wasn't a prayer, exactly, but God was still listening. A week passes. Then Jesus is suddenly there with them *(even though the doors were locked.)* Jesus confronts Thomas and his fears and doubts face to face, answering his prayer (of sorts) in the most tangible (tactile?) of ways:

> *Then he said to Thomas, "Put your finger here;*
> *see my hands. Reach out your hand and put*
> *it in my side. Stop doubting and believe."*
> *John 20:27 (NIV)*

We are timid and doubting creatures, sometimes doubting that God will do what He said, but often doubting that we have heard from God at all. "Was that really you God?" seems to be one of my most frequent prayers. I should just save time and start abbreviating it in my journal —"WTRYG?" You too? Yeah, I see you.

I'm especially intrigued by Moses' interaction with God in Exodus 24:16-18 *(NIV):*

> *For six days the cloud covered the mountain,*
> *and on the SEVENTH day the LORD called to*
> *Moses from within the cloud. To the Israelites,*

81

> *the Glory of the LORD looked like a consuming*
> *fire on top of the mountain. Then Moses*
> *entered the Cloud as he went up the mountain.*
> *And he stayed on the mountain forty days and*
> *forty nights...*

God called to Moses out of the cloud. But Moses didn't just hang out with Joshua and wait another seven days for God to speak again. He *ENTERED THE FIRECLOUD* to be with God. I am reminded of the three men thrown in the furnace in the book of Daniel, yet the king cried out that he saw *FOUR* men walking around in the furnace, "and the fourth looks like a son of the gods!" We believers tend to think that following God should eliminate problems in our lives. That God is going to pull us out of the fire. Not necessarily so. Zechariah 13:8-9 *(NIV)* reads:

> *In the whole land," declares the LORD, "two-*
> *thirds will be struck down and perish, yet one*
> *third will be left in it. This third **I WILL***
> ***BRING INTO THE FIRE**; I will refine them*
> *like silver and test them like gold. They will call*
> *on my name and I will answer them; I will say,*
> *'They are my people,' and they will say, 'The*
> *LORD is our God.'*

Sometimes God reaches out his hand to take ours and walk with us through a fiery cloud – a firestorm. Flames are all around, and the burning embers are swirling through the air in a great dance. Everything's on fire. But God is there. If this is you, I pray grace and courage on you as you hold God's hand and keep walking. And waiting. And lingering in His presence.

Even if your whole world is on fire.

47. Helping God Out

I'm reading this morning in Numbers 20. The People of Israel have arrived in the Desert of Zin and found (to their surprise?) that there was no water there, and nothing especially nice to eat. Their first response was teenager-rhetorical. *"I wish I was DEAD."* Their second response was to gripe about their current situation and look back longingly to Egypt, that *WONDERFUL* place where they were slaves for 400 years. Ah yes, the good old days..

Moses and Aaron took the problem to God, who gave Moses very specific instructions. He was to take the staff in his hand and *SPEAK* to the rock, and water would come out. (In a similar situation roughly 40 years previous, Exodus 17 tells us that God told Moses to *STRIKE* the rock. He did so, and water came out.)

Moses takes the staff, gathers the people, stomps his foot (probably), and gives his little speech:

> *Listen you rebels! Must we bring you water out*
> *of this rock?" Then Moses raised his arm and*
> *struck the rock twice with his staff. Water*
> *gushed out, and the community and*
> *their livestock drank...*
> *Numbers 20:10-11 (NIV)*

SUCCESS! Water came out, and everyone was happy. Everyone except God, that is. God pulled Moses and Aaron aside and told them something incredibly chilling in verse 12:

Because you did not TRUST me enough to
honor me as Holy in the sight of the Israelites,
YOU will not bring this community into the
land I give them.

Moses decided to help God out, by striking the rock. You know, just to make sure the water came out. (Was he worried about loss of face if he spoke to the rock, and nothing happened?) And besides, this method worked spectacularly in the past-- God even told him to do it that way, and God *BLESSED* it! But God wanted to do a *NEW* thing. Striking the rock this time (sticking with the tried and true?), was disobedience driven by lack of trust, and this was a public offense against God's Holiness. In response, God canceled the future He had planned for them. Wow.

I don't know about you, but I want everything God has planned for me. And I *PROMISE* you, there have been times where I have tried to strike the rock. To help God out. You know, just to make *SURE* I got the desired result. And these times I am thinking of were *EPIC* failures. Worse, I offended God's Holiness through my disobedience driven by my lack of trust.

So my prayer now, is that I will *TRUST* God and rigorously obey. But obey out of love and childlike trust, not fear. That I will honor God as holy through that active trust. And that I will never try to help God out again! It is that I will embrace the NEW thing that God has us doing---

Even though it might look very different from the way God had us doing Ministry in the past.

48.   Say the Name

My wife is out of town and, as is typical for sleeping without her, I was awake for much of the night. So this morning I was praying and journaling about a dream, and about some other things God showed me last night. And then God brought a Margaret Becker song to mind. Margaret Becker's music was a huge influence on my spiritual life years ago. I loved her heart. Her sincerity. Her transparency in seeking God. This is the song God picked for me that day. It's called *Say the Name*:

> *Say the name- Jesus!*
> *Say the name that soothes the soul*
> *The name of gentle healing*
> *And peace immutable*
>
> *Say the name*
> *That has heard my cry*
> *Has seen my tears*
> *And wiped them dry*
> *From now until the end of time*
> *I'll say the name.*[16]

Are you hurting right now? Concerned about the future? Grieving the past? All the above? Same.

Say The Name.

---

[16] Charlie Peacock, Margaret Becker, *Say the Name,* album Soul 1993, track 3, produced by Charlie Peacock, Sparrow Records, Brentwood TN, https://www.youtube.com/watch?v=DsNHtw7ZT-c

49. Enter the Silence

I was reading in Lamentations chapter 3 in *The Message* tonight, and verse 25 really grabbed me.

> *GOD proves to be good to the man who*
> *passionately waits,*
> > *to the woman who diligently seeks.*

What does it mean to *PASSIONATELY* wait? I wonder... Is it to actively anticipate that God will act? It reminds me of Psalm 130:5-6, quoted from the *NIV*:

> *I wait for the LORD, my soul waits,*
> > *and in his word I put my hope.*
> *My soul waits for the Lord*
> *more than watchmen wait for the morning,*
> *more than watchmen wait for the morning.*

I'm picturing the sentry on the city wall, listening to noises in the dark. Wondering if the enemy is approaching. Fatigued. Waiting for the dawn when he can see clearly. When his relief arrives, he can rest, so he is constantly glancing at the eastern sky. Is it growing lighter? Is dawn approaching?

> *My soul waits for the Lord,*
> *more than watchmen wait for the morning,*
> *more than watchmen wait for the morning.*

Back in Jeremiah 3, verse 28 reads:

> *When life is heavy and hard to take,*
> *go off by yourself.*
>
> *Enter the silence.*

86

Moses would go to the Tent of Meeting. Why do you think they called it that? Because that's where you went to meet with God. So many times, Jesus went to a solitary place to pray. The last such place he chose was a garden called Gethsemane. A quiet place.

Do you have a special place you go to, to enter the silence? Mine is a place called Pigeon Point, in Beaufort SC, with the best sunsets in town. I go there with Bible, journal, and guitar. I call it my crying place. I go there to meet with God, and to worship him there. To write songs, and to enter the silence.

> *When life is heavy and hard to take,*
> *go off by yourself.*
>
> *Enter the silence.*

50. Roads You Travel

Psalm 84:5-7 in *The Message* reads:

> *And how blessed all those in whom You live,*
> *whose lives become roads You travel;*
>
> *They wind through lonesome valleys, come*
> *upon brooks,*
> *discover cool springs and pools brimming with*
> *rain!*
>
> *God-traveled, these roads curve up the*
> *mountain,*
> *and at the last turn – Zion! God in full view!*

Sometimes God shows us things he wants to do in our lives. It's like looking through a telescopic camera lens or binoculars at a mountain range. Distance is compressed, and we think we are seeing a single mountain. We hike that road and turn the corner, thinking we're almost there! Except... there is another peak in the distance and the road drops into a valley. Ugh.

But it's God's road. And this road through the lonely valley has surprises at strategic places-- cool springs, and pools of rainwater to rest by. Even better, it's written that God himself travels these roads!

> *And how blessed all those in whom You live,*
> *whose lives become roads You travel;*

In Luke 24 (quoting from *The Message*) we encounter two men walking on a lonely road. They were heavy burdened because their master, Jesus of Nazareth, had just been executed. All hope was gone. And to add insult, someone had stolen his body. I expect this was a very lonely road indeed!

> *In the middle of their talk and questions, Jesus*
> *came up and walked along with them. But they*
> *were not able to recognize who he was...*

Jesus talked with them as they walked, pointing out everything in the scripture about himself, how the Messiah HAD to suffer, and only then enter into his glory. They arrived, sat down for a meal.

> *Taking the bread, he blessed and broke and*
> *gave it to them. At that moment, open-eyed,*
> *wide-eyed, they recognized him...*

I personally tend to be in a hurry. I eat and drive. I eat while I walk. I prefer cookies to cake because I can eat them on the go. Cake requires a plate and a fork, and stillness to enjoy it. Some believers just want to get to heaven. To *BE* there already, away from this irksome life. But God wants to walk on this road with us. To show us little surprises on the way. Not to snap his fingers and have us immediately at the end of our journey. No! He has plans for us! Divine encounters, and pleasant surprises.

John 21 tells us that after the crucifixion and Resurrection, the disciples had gone fishing. They had fished all night and caught nothing. They were skunked, as my Uncle Jeff would say. At sunrise, there was Jesus on the beach. "Catch anything?" Um... not really, no.

"Throw the net on the other side of the boat!" he shouted. Right. But they did it, and suddenly their net was full of fish! After they drug the net ashore, they saw Jesus already had bread and fish cooking. Breakfast was ready. Provision had already been made, and it was time to sit down and eat. To loiter in his presence.

Friends, as we walk this road, let's not be in a hurry. Let's enjoy the sights and hang out with Jesus when we encounter him. "Coffee with Jesus", as author Lana Vawser puts it.

Enjoy the journey.

51. The Fatherhood Mission

I opened this morning to Hosea 1 and started reflecting on God's timetable and the (unglamorous?) missions he assigns us.

The very first recorded time God spoke to his prophet Hosea, He told him to get married and have children. And so he does. She gets pregnant, they have a son, and God names him. She gets pregnant again and has a daughter. God names her. After the baby was weaned (two years? three years? four?) she gets pregnant again and they have another son. God names that boy also and begins to speak to Hosea at length. So this is three pregnancies and a weaning. So what is that-- four to seven years? During this time frame – crying babies, sleepless nights ("Mommy? Mommy? Mommy? Mommy?") it is only recorded that God spoke to his prophet on three occasions – the birth of each child.

Why?

Because it was not yet his mission to be a prophet to the nations. His mission from God was *TO LOVE THAT WOMAN AND BE A FATHER* to their children. That was his mission. To Father those children and love their mother. No matter what. (Hosea 3:1.)

The scripture records another man who was given such a fatherhood mission. His name was Joseph. He was engaged to a woman named Mary. But then she got pregnant. Even worse, the baby wasn't his! Disaster upon disaster. But God told him to go ahead with the wedding, and God used him to protect that woman and that child – God's *OWN* Son – from all dangers.

This was his mission! To be a *FATHER* to that child, and to love that child's mother.

So you men out there – are you a Father? Then you already have a mission from God, and it's a worthy one. Father them. Do you love a woman who comes with kids from a previous relationship? They're your kids too now. Father them.

Do you have a "calling from God" on your life? Not sure? What if this is it? Could it be, that like Joseph, God's primary calling on your life is to be a father to those children-- maybe even another man's children, and to love their mother? And those children will go on to do incredible things? (Hat tip to all the wonderful fathers I know who married a woman who already came with children, or adopted some along the way. Instant family. Men like Michael Holliday, Jonathan Kalkan, Gabriel Holliday, Jeff Hughes, David Sage, Zayden Weinert, Butch Mills, and Neil E. Hurley. You guys are my heroes.) What a mission!

Happy Father's Day.

52.   The Day the Lord Has Made

Meet Romanian pastor Richard Wurmbrand! In the YouTube video, "Richard and Sabina Wurmbrand Interview in 1989" https://www.youtube.com/watch?v=helKvd5ymeE, he shares at the 11:30 mark about the musical instruments their captors courteously provided them. Their chains!

[Singing]
This is the day! [clink-clink-clink]
That the Lord has made [clink-clink-clink-
clink]
We will rejoice [clink]
And be glad in it [clink-clink-clink-clink.]
...
"This is the day that the Lord has made – a day
of beating. A day of torture. A day of hunger. A
day of deprivation of everything. A day of not
knowing if you have a wife. If you have a
mother. If the children have not died. You have
nothing. But I have a task. A task to bring a
song in this sadness..."
...
"I have been a lucky fellow. Only fourteen
years in jail!"

Then he proceeds to name others, jailed 40 years and counting...

"Suffering offers two possibilities: either you
can become BITTER,
         or you can become BETTER..."
                                  -Richard Wurmbrand

Wow.

53. Storm-Tossed

A picture came up on OneDrive from two years ago. This shoreline had been ravaged by a recent hurricane, but this one tree was still standing. As I was looking at it, John 12:27-28 came to mind, quoted from *The Message*:

> *Right now I am storm-tossed. And what am I going to say, "Father get me out of this"? No, this is why I came in the first place. I'll say, "Father, put your glory on display."*

Jesus had just come into Jerusalem to joyous crowds, loud Hosannas, and palm branches. But instead of planning his expected coronation, he started to talk about his execution.

Wait – *WHAT?!?!*

Jesus knew what was coming. He *KNEW*. But instead of opting out of this horrendous trial, this great pain, he asked instead that God the Father showcase His Glory in the process. Either we are storm-tossed right now, or we will be. It's been said that *"Sometimes Jesus calms the storm, but other times he lets the storm rage and calms his child."* I think the latter is more common.

So God, whatever happens today, or tomorrow, or for all the rest of my tomorrows – please calm my heart, give me courage, and put your Glory on display...

54.   The Outsider

This has been percolating a bit, and I wanted to both share it and make sense of it at the same time. Those of you who know me well will remember that I tend to think out loud and to reason through things with others. So please bear with me.

In Acts chapter 8, God set up a divine appointment for Phillip, by telling him to take a hike. Literally. God told him to go south to the road, the desert road, that leads from Jerusalem to Gaza. Gaza was about 50 miles away. Did God want him to walk all the way there, through the desert??? This was a pretty open-ended bit of instruction!

(As an aside, I have two teenagers living at home. One requires 15 minutes notice to pack for a three-day road-trip. The other wants to know every blessed detail of an afternoon spent with Dad. When will we leave? Where exactly will we go, and in what order? What will we do at each place? And how long will we linger per stop? I tend to function spiritually like the second one, constantly asking God for answers about *EVERYTHING*. But God is telling me to *TRUST* him and just get in the car.)

Phillip sets out, and bumps into an important eunuch, the Minister of Finance for the Queen of Ethiopia. He had gone to Jerusalem to worship and was on his way home. He had taken a rest stop from the bumpy road and was taking the time to read. Philip approached the chariot at God's nudging and heard the Ethiopian reading aloud. In Isaiah 53. *INTERESTING!* Philip jumps right in (see what I did there?,) asks him if he understands what he is reading, and then starts to explain the passage to him at the man's request.

This Ethiopian was an Outsider. He didn't fit. Had the wrong skin color and a foreign accent. He didn't belong there. But worse, he had a very personal problem – he had been castrated. His genitals had been mutilated to keep him loyal and subservient, which now led to a *religious* problem. He had gone to Jerusalem to worship, but had likely been refused entry into the temple. The Law of Moses in Deuteronomy 23:1 *(NIV)* states:

> *No one whose testicles are crushed or whose*
> *male organ is cut off shall enter the assembly of*
> *the LORD.*

He WANTED to worship God, but the church had a big Keep Out sign posted for his kind. But had he read a little further in Isaiah, he would have come to chapter 56, which had been written specifically for him – the ultimate outsider. I am quoting here from *The Message*:

> *Make sure no outsider who now follows God*
> *ever has occasion to say, "God put me in*
> *second-class. I don't really belong."*

> *And make sure no physically mutilated person*
> *is ever made to think, "I'm damaged goods. I*
> *don't really belong."*

> *For GOD says:*

> *"To the eunuchs who keep my Sabbaths, who*
> *choose what pleases me and hold fast to my*
> *covenant – to them I will give **within** my temple*
> *and it's walls a memorial and a name better*

*than sons and daughters; I will give them an
everlasting name **that will not be cut off.**"*

Unlike their lost manhood.

Notice the line about Damaged Goods. Have you ever felt that way? Maybe you have been in prison? Lost your virginity to someone, but now they are long gone, and you are ready to get married and settle down, but are afraid your new love won't want you if they can't be your first? Or maybe you are single and lonely, and you want to get married, but you already have kids? Maybe you're a pregnant teenager? Divorced? Had an abortion? Been to drug rehab? Alcoholic? Homeless?

There are lots of ways to be an outsider, and it's way too easy to be shunned by the church. But I am also thinking about school shootings. How many of the school shooters were outsiders? Loners? New to the school? Kids who didn't fit in, didn't dress like other kids, or didn't hang out with the others? Kids who were bullied? How many fit this description? How many were outsiders?

All of them.

Our job then is to welcome the outsider. The mutilated. The weirdos. The ex-cons. The single moms. The tatted up. The immigrant. Get to know them. Talk to them and be their friend. See where it goes!

> *To the mutilated who keep my Sabbaths and
> choose what delights me and keep a firm
> grip on my covenant, I'll provide them an
> honored place in my family and within my city,
> even more honored than that of sons*

and daughters. I'll confer permanent honors on
them that will never be revoked.
- Isaiah 56:4-5, NIV

55.   Children Who Rocked the World

I have been ruminating this morning on children's ministry and
youth ministry. The Bible and secular history have a number of
examples of child monarchs who had tremendous influence on
history, for good or evil:

- *Joash, age 7 – renovated the Temple*
- *Uzziah, age 16 – strengthened the defenses.*
  Reigned 52 years.
- *Manasseh, age 12 – led his nation into*
  practices of evil far beyond that of the
  surrounding nations God had previously
  destroyed.
- *Josiah, age 8 – cleansed the country and*
  Temple of idol worship

And here are a few of my favorites from secular history:

- *Tutankhamun, age 9 – restored ancient*
  monuments and moved the capital of Egypt
- *Mehmed The Conqueror, age 12 –*
  Captured Constantinople at age 21. At that
  moment, he spoke Turkish, Arabic, Persian,
  Greek, and Latin. (He taught himself
  Serbian later.)
- *Alexander the Great, age 20 – conquered*
  the world.

- *Mary, Queen of Scots, crowned at 6 days old – first female ruler of Scotland, married to the King of France, fought with Elizabeth I to rule England.*

So, these children, these "young PEOPLE," assumed great power at a young age. Their character and actions were strongly influenced, not just by their parents, but by their teachers.

Children's Ministry *MATTERS.*

Youth Ministry *MATTERS.*

School Teachers *MATTER.*

So if you are working with children, teenagers, or young adults, your ministry is not a sideline. Not an also-ran. It is *IMPORTANT.* Yes it's hard. Yes it can be discouraging.

Don't quit.

56. "Trust My Timing"

FYI, I am a Grade-A Worrywart. Often I worry about fitting all the puzzle pieces together, and especially about timing. I keep trying to reason through things, but lately, God has been saying to me over and over,

"Trust My Timing."

And then, to emphasize the point, He has been showing me an incredibly beautiful bronze pocket watch. The cover is exquisitely engraved with beautiful writing (which I can't read.) But most interestingly, the cover is partially cut away to reveal the face of the clock below. But *ONLY* from 12 o'clock to 2 o'clock is visible. Like a pizza slice taken out. The hands of the clock are somewhere else under the cover. So, I know the time is between 2:00 pm and midnight. Helpful!

God is emphasizing that he is *DELIBERATELY* covering the hands of the clock because I don't *GET* to know the time. He wants me to *TRUST* him, and *just live my life...*

In Matthew 21, Jesus curses the fig tree, and his disciples were astonished to find it withered the very next day. Which is not at all the natural order of things. What they didn't understand is that God stands outside of time. He can speed it up and slow it down at will.

There's a really great scene in *The Voyage of The Dawn Treader*, by C.S. Lewis, in which our heroine Lucy is having an intimate conversation with the great lion Aslan, and she asks him, "What do you call 'Soon,' Aslan?" He replies simply, "I call all times soon." [17]

"So God," I ask in the here and now, *"when will* [X, Y, Z] *happen?"*

"Soon."

Hahahahahaha! Perfect.

"Trust My Timing."

---

[17] C. S. Lewis, *The Voyage of the Dawn Treader* (London: Geoffrey Bles, 1952)

57. No Locked Doors

In Numbers 12, Moses was having family problems. His brother and sister were gossiping because they didn't like his new foreign wife. (Was she young, hot, and half his age? Did they disapprove of his new interracial marriage?) And then they started saying things like "Doesn't God speak through us too?" (Who does he think he is?!?!?) God ordered the three of them to the Tent of Meeting for a family intervention.

I would have pointed out that Moses was the leader *I* chose, and that he could marry whomever he pleased! But no. Instead, God commented on the level of intimacy Moses enjoyed with him.

> *When there is a prophet among you, I, the LORD, reveal myself to them in visions, I speak to them in dreams. But this is not true of my servant Moses; he is faithful in all my house. With him I speak face to face, clearly and not in riddles; he sees the form of the LORD. Why then were you not afraid to speak against my servant Moses?" (NIV)*

God pointed out that his *USUAL* method of communication with his prophets is in dreams and visions. In puzzles. In riddles – things that are hard to understand. Why? Because it forces us to seek Him for the answers. But Moses was SO close to Him, that they talked face to face. And God pointed out something especially interesting. *"He is faithful in all my house."* This phrase has connotations of Trust. Like when a business owner has a general manager that is so competent and trusted, the owner doesn't need to continuously look over their shoulder.

This is how it was with Joseph running Egypt under Pharaoh. Most English translations word it as *"he is faithful in all my house."* But I am intrigued by how *The Message* says it:

> *He has the run of my entire house.*

There were no locked doors. No wings were roped off. No hidden basements. No areas where Moses was not allowed to be or know about. No secrets. This is where I want to be. A level of intimacy with God where there are no secrets, and no locked doors. Where God has *FULL ACCESS* to my life. Where we just talk back and forth as intimate friends. But until that point, there are still riddles I am asking about!

So friends, I am asking God that He will give us a hunger for intimacy with Him – that talking with him will be our last conscious thought as we sleep at night, and our first thought as we wake up. I'm not there yet.

(But I want to be.)

58. To the Moon

Sara Groves wrote the thought-provoking song *To the Moon* about Christian Escapism:

> *It was there in the bulletin we're leaving soon*
> *After the bake sale to raise funds for fuel*
> *The rocket is ready and we're going to*
> *Take our church to the moon*

> *There'll be no one there to tell us we're odd*
> *No one to change our opinion of God*
> *Just lots of rocks and this dusty sod*

Here at our church on the moon

We know our liberties we know our rights
We know how to fight a very good fight
Just get that last bag and turn out the light
We're taking our church to the moon
We're taking our church to the moon
We'll be leaving soon[18]

Many Christians in America tend to mentally divide the world into sacred and secular. Jobs like pastors and priests and missionaries are sacred. Jobs like politician, construction worker, and soldier are secular. But here's the thing. God *WANTS* to be involved in every aspect of our lives. Our jobs, our marriages, our recreation, our sex lives, our child-rearing, and even our politics. **Pro Tip:** it's *ALL* Sacred.

Over a millennia ago, some Christians took the concept of *"set apart as holy"* to extreme lengths, building monasteries way out in the desert, to get away from this wicked world so as to be "more holy." A few ascetics, the stylites, lived on top of columns for the ultimate self-denial experience. Disciples would send food up and the stylite would presumably defecate over the edge. The devout would come on pilgrimage to see the "holy man", and hopefully catch some of his holiness? (One stylite reportedly stayed up there 67 years.)

We chuckle at the thought of such silliness, but we do it too! I know Christians who grew up in church, went to a Christian

---

[18] Sara Groves , To The Moon, album Add to the Beauty, 2005, track 9, produced by Brown Bannister, INO Records/Fair Trade Services, Brentwood TN, https://www.youtube.com/watch?v=nUKk8p3Kyko

school Kindergarten through-12th grade, went to a Christian college and work for a church ministry. They play ball in their local church league, take their kids to the church athletic program, and are in church Sunday morning, Sunday night and Wednesday night. Plus they go to Bible studies and home groups and women's ministries and men's ministries on other nights. There is something you can do at church every day of the week. So really, their only exposure to people not exactly like them may be at the grocery store or on the television!

But it's *all* sacred. God wants it all. We like using the phrase "dirty politics" because it makes us feel morally superior. We want to be left alone. To not get involved. But do you want to know how to get left alone? *It's by getting involved.* Hahahaha! Getting involved allows you to affect which local laws and ordinances are made so that you ARE left alone; so that you are free to practice you faith without government interference. The Bible is filled with examples of God-fearers who *were* involved and had huge impact by having the ear of rulers, and sometimes by being in authority themselves.

Genesis 41:45 (MSG) tells us that Joseph had such a profound impact on Pharoah that he not only leapfrogged everyone in the country on the career ladder, but also that Pharaoh gave him a new name and a wife from a powerful family. And get this – the name Pharaoh gave him meant "**God - Speaks - And - He - Lives.**" Dude! Have *YOU* ever been given a name that emphasizes a relationship with the living God? And I expect the woman was young and drop-dead gorgeous. I mean, Pharaoh wouldn't reward his new best friend by marrying him off to an unattractive woman? No, she was definitely a keeper. Much like my own wife, created special for me!

In 1 Samuel 29:6 *(NIV)*, the Philistine king Achish of Gath, releases David from his service by saying "as God *LIVES*, you have been a trusted ally..." Just like in Joseph's naming ceremony, here we have a pagan ruler honoring The Living God, specifically because of their close personal connection to one of God's servants. Some other examples of secular rulers influenced by God-followers include King Xerxes (Esther and Mordecai), Balak (Balaam), King Nebuchadnezzar (Daniel and his three friends), King Artaxerxes (Nehemiah, his cup bearer), King Belshazzar (Daniel), King Darius (Daniel), King Cyrus (again Daniel), the King of Nineveh (Jonah), King Herod (John the Baptist), and Governor Pilate (Jesus). Paul spoke before governors Gallio, Felix, and Festus, King Agrippa, and Emperor Nero.

So get involved! Vote. Run for office. Be in politics. Join the YMCA. Be in clubs. Meet the neighbors. Go to Town Council and School Board meetings. Be part of this world!

It's all sacred.

59. Suffering and the Believer

This morning I am really struck by the struggles of king Hezekiah. In the book of 2 Chronicles, chapters 29-31 tell how he became king at age 25, and in the very first month of his reign he started purifying and repairing the Temple. Then he brought the whole country together to reestablish the Temple sacrifices, and to celebrate Passover together as a nation. They got rid of idols and the people brought in tithes and offerings. He was doing great things for God!

And yet, chapter 32, quoted from *The New International Version,* opens with this horrific assessment:

> *After all that Hezekiah had so faithfully done, Sennacherib king of Assyria came and invaded Judah...*

We American Christians tend to think of pain and trouble as God's punishment for wrongdoing, or his correction to bring us back to him. And it *CAN* be, to be sure. But here we have a dream- king, doing absolutely everything right – and then *NATIONAL DISASTER*. Wait, what?

Sometimes God allows suffering in our lives, so that He will be glorified in our response, in our trust in Him, regardless of the pain. So what did Hezekiah do? He begged God for divine intervention, but he also did everything he could to get ready for the coming storm by preparing their defenses and stocking up on supplies. Some might ask, "But why didn't he just ask God to save them?"

I am reminded of the story of the man in the flood who climbed up on his roof to await rescue. A boat came by, but he refused to get in, citing his reliance on God to save him. A second boat came, and then a third. Nope. Trusting God! Then, a helicopter came, but he waived them off too. Finally, the house was carried away and he drowned. In heaven, the perplexed man asked God, *"But why didn't you save me?!?"* God responded with, *"I sent you three boats and a helicopter!"*

In Hezekiah's case, God *DID* save them, but not until other cities had been conquered, and many Godfearing citizens killed. Two years of famine and scarcity still followed the destruction of the enemy army at the hand of the Lord; pain, suffering, and hard times were all around.

Sunday morning a week ago, God woke me up in the early morning with a very significant dream. In the dream, I saw dark grey storm clouds coming toward me. They looked boiling, as though they were an ash cloud from a volcanic eruption. Every bit of sky was covered. It was all-encompassing. As I watched, a huge bolt of lightning struck the center of the road, right in front of me. Then I woke up. Immediately, I understood the interpretation.

The Storm is almost here.

My friends, I work on the water, and I watch the sky. When I see clouds and lightning *THIS* close, it has my immediate attention. It is time to either moveout or hunkerdown. I firmly believe the storm of war is coming to us here in the USA. Please, beg God for mercy, but prepare for hard times.

May the LORD answer you
when you are in distress;
may the name of the God
of Jacob protect you.
***
Some trust in chariots
and some in horses,
but we trust in the name
of the LORD our God.
-Psalm 20:1,7 (NIV)

Strength and courage! (and stock up!)

60. Times of Pain

Some spiritual moments are beautiful, but some are hard and bitter, coming from a place of pain. Musician and songwriter Michael Card writes in his book *A Sacred Sorrow*:

> *From the beginning, David was no stranger to pain. And in the end, it was the process of lamenting his pain that led him to an unheard-of intimacy with God. From his pen flowed the intimate words of suffering that Jesus would one day use in giving voice to His own pain on the cross. Through the words of these laments, God would redeem a mountain of sin and spiritual suffering. Through his Psalms of Lament, as perhaps nowhere else in Scripture, David reveals a God who uses and utilizes everything, especially pain. All true songs of worship are born in the wilderness of suffering. It is the pen of pain that writes those songs that call us forth to dance. David, like no one else, suffered and danced throughout the stumbling course of the rocky terrain of his lonely life.* [19]

This really resonates with me. I have found in my own attempts at songwriting, the best ones have come from places of pain. Moments like in 2 Kings 19, where all the fortified cities of

---

[19] Michael Card, *A Sacred Sorrow: Reaching out to God in the Lost Language of Lament* (Colorado Springs CO, NavPress, 2005)

Judah have fallen and Hezekiah, in tears, runs to the Temple and spreads Sennacherib's ultimatum letter out on the Altar before the Lord. Times of pain.

Psalm 74, in the *NIV* tells us:

> *Your foes roared in the place where you met*
> *with us.*
> > *They set up their standards as signs.*
> *They behaved like men wielding axes*
> > *to cut through a thicket of trees.*
> *They smashed all the carved paneling*
> > *with their axes and hatchets.*
> *They burned your sanctuary to the ground;*
> *they defiled the dwelling place of your Name.*
> > *They said in their hearts,*
> *"We will crush them completely!"*
> > *They burned every place*
> *Where God was worshipped in the land.*

And worst of all, perhaps:

> *We are given no miraculous signs,*
> *no prophets are left,*
> *and none of us knows how long this will be.*

One is reminded of Jesus' cry of anguish on the cross, quoting David in Psalm 22:1:

> *My God, my God, why have you forsaken me?*
> *(NIV).*

Commentaries suggest that the Lament of Psalm 74 refers to the fall of Jerusalem to the Babylonians, but there are many examples of believers slaughtered in their houses of worship. When Constantinople fell to the Ottomans on May 29, 1453, thousands of citizens fled to the great cathedral Hagia Sophia for refuge. Most of the elderly and infirm were killed. The younger ones, both sexes, were raped. Then they were sold naked into slavery. And each of these sufferers called on the name of Jesus.

Years ago, I had the privilege of visiting Vardzia, in the Republic of Georgia in the Caucasus mountains. Incidentally, Georgia claims to be the world's first Christian kingdom. (As does Armenia, next door.) In the 12th century, queen Tamar built this secret underground fortress, with 13 levels, 6,000 rooms, and space for 50,000 citizens to take refuge from the Mongols. It was the ultimate prepper bugout location.

A century later however, an earthquake destroyed two-thirds of it and left the remaining caves exposed to the sunlight and to their enemies. I'm sure there was a whole lot of lamenting going on after that catastrophe. A dear friend once told me that her favorite word was "Alas!" and that word fits their situation perfectly. Their defenses gone, all their carefully made plans and preparations, defeated in moments. Alas!

As I admired the murals on the church wall, I noticed and commented on the great iron door. The monk pointed out the window at a boulder and replied simply "on that stone Shah Abbas slew 30 monks." Then he took me behind the altar, behind a richly woven tapestry, and uncovered a narrow escape tunnel, winding its way through the mountain. It was full of side tunnels and hidden overhead compartments *"where arrows could be shot at pursuers."* It was like something out of *The Lord of the Rings*. But this was real life. Real Christian History.

We think Christians really shouldn't suffer. If we are in pain, something must be wrong, right? In Matthew 16 in *The Message* tells us:

> *Then Jesus went to work on his disciples.*
> *"Anyone who intends to come after me has to*
> *let me lead. You're not in the driver's seat; I*
> *am. Don't run from suffering; embrace it.*
> *Follow me and I will show you how..."*

My friends, I believe suffering is coming. Suffering beyond that of ordinary life here in easy- living America. Maybe even in our houses of worship, our beautiful Hagia Sophias. But my prayer is that we sit with each other in our suffering, and bear one another's burdens. And that our heart's response will be that of Job. To worship.

> *At this, Job got up and tore his robe and shaved*
> *his head. Then he fell to the ground in*
> *WORSHIP and said:*
> *"Naked I came from my mother's womb, and*
> *naked I will depart. The LORD gave, and the*
> *LORD has taken away; may the Name of the*
> *LORD be praised."*
>
> *-Job 1:20-21 (NIV)*

61.   Patience in the Waiting

I noticed something this morning for the first time, and it really grabbed me. In Acts chapters 18 and 19, we find Paul and his friends in Ephesus. We are familiar with the bonfire of witchcraft books, joyfully burned by their former owners as they became acquainted with the living God. And we are familiar with the silversmith riot, where the silversmiths brought the whole city into an uproar at the stadium, threatening to lynch Paul and his companions. All because these new believers stopped buying the god-images they were selling, and it was hurting their wallets. Good times.

But what we miss is the time factor. Acts 18 tells us that Paul first arrived in Ephesus with Priscilla and Aquila, stayed briefly, then left them behind and sailed to Caesarea and then Antioch, where he spent "considerable time." Paul eventually returned to Ephesus.

> *Paul then went straight to the meeting place. He had the run of the place for three months, doing his best to make the things of the kingdom of God real and convincing to them. But then resistance began to form as some of them began spreading evil rumors through the congregation about the Christian way of life. So Paul left, taking the disciples with him, and set up shop in the school of Tyrannus, holding class there daily. He did this for two years, giving everyone in the province of Asia, Jews as well as Greeks, ample opportunity to hear the Message of the Master.*
> *-Acts 19:8-10, The Message*

So, "considerable time", plus "three months", plus "two years" of normal everyday life and ministry before the big flashy results. (I really don't like the way this is trending!) I want Christian life to be more like TV crime shows. Stuff happens, it is investigated, and the mystery is solved. Everything is wrapped up in 40 minutes, plus commercials. I ask God for answers, or for breakthrough, and expect replies in TV time.

Except... God doesn't usually work that way. He takes his time. *HIS* time. *Often YEARS.* So be patient. Keep plodding. We worship **The - God - Whose - Timing - Is - Perfect**.

Be patient. And be at peace in the waiting.

62. Tread Lightly

Tonight I'm pondering the fear of God. Not in the normal Christian lexicon sense of *"God may smite me!"*, but more along the lines of *"God, you're frightening me-- please stop???"*

In Mark chapter 5, quoted from the *NIV*, we are told that Jesus encountered a demonized man who lived among the tombs and was so wild that:

> *No man could bind him, even with a chain. For*
> *he had often been chained hand and foot, but*
> *he tore the chains apart and broke the irons*
> *on his feet. No one was strong enough to*
> *subdue him. Night and day among the tombs*
> *and in the hills he would cry out and cut*
> *himself with stones...*

He ran to Jesus and the demons inside spoke to Jesus and begged him to allow them to go into the nearby heard of pigs instead of sending them completely away.

He gave them permission, and the evil spirits
came out and went into the pigs. The herd,
about two thousand in number, rushed down
the steep bank into the lake and were drowned.

Okay, so demons were talking with raspy voices and there was lots of thrashing around, just like in your favorite exorcist-type movie. But now we get to the *REALLY* scary part:

Those tending the pigs ran off and reported this
in the town and the countryside, and the people
went out to see what had happened. When they
came to Jesus, they saw the man who had been
possessed by the legion of demons, sitting
there, dressed and in his right mind; and they
were afraid...

The kingdom of God was among them. Not demonstrated by violence, *but by PEACE.* Such an extreme change in this man required such a demonstration of power that they were *AFRAID.* (What might Jesus decide to change in their own lives too, if they let Him get too close?)

And so they asked Him, no, they *BEGGED* Him, to leave. So He did.

There may come a day when God shows up in our comfortable church service and makes us uncomfortable. *Very* uncomfortable. Just with His Holy Presence, or in the way He is doing something in someone or through someone. *"But God, that's just not how we do things here!"*

> *Forget the former things;*
>   *do not dwell on the past.*
> *See, I am doing a new thing!*
>   *Now it springs up; do you not perceive it?*
>   *-Isaiah 43:18-19 (NIV)*

Tread lightly friends.

63.   Though the fig tree does not blossom...

I had a friend once who had a plaque with a quote attributed to John Wayne. *"Life is tough. But it's tougher if you're stupid."* I like that. Partly because it suggests if you're smart, *i.e., NOT* stupid, you can better your life. That's the conceit that keeps me self-employed. That if I'm smart and diligent, I can be successful. But what if that's not enough? What if I'm smart and diligent, but my life is still a disaster? Some people say hard times make the man, while others suggest that hard times *REVEAL* the man. I think there is some truth in both statements. But sometimes, our life falls apart in spite of hard work and good choices.

Habakkuk 3:17-19 addresses a national-level calamity. Foreign invasion and famine, in spite of best efforts. The description of the disaster is eloquent, and the writer's response is epic:

> *Though the fig tree does not bud*
> *and there are no grapes on the vines,*
> *though the olive crop fails*
> *and the fields produce no food,*

though there are no sheep in the pen
and no cattle in the stalls,
yet I will rejoice in the LORD,
I will be joyful in God my Savior.

The Sovereign LORD is my strength;
he makes my feet like the feet of a deer, he
enables me to go on the heights.

For the director of music. On my stringed
instruments.

This was quoted from the *New International Version*, the *NIV*. But I noticed the *King James Version* I grew up with has a critically different nuance. Where the *NIV* states from the shepherd's perspective that there are no sheep in the pen (economic ruin) the *King James Version* says, *"the flock shall be cut off from the fold."* This is a disaster from the **SHEEP's** perspective. The sheep fold was shelter from the elements and protection from predators. Once inside and the door was shut, they were safe. But here it says they are cut off from the fold. In the wind. Homeless. In danger from hungry predators. In exile.

Awhile back, God showed me just such a scene. I saw a ragged gaggle of people – 15-20 maybe. They were walking down the street in small-town America. All the houses were dark and deserted. A convenience store had the door hanging off its hinges, and it had been thoroughly looted. The group came to a crossroads, had a discussion among themselves, and decided to turn left. It looked like a scene out of *The Walking Dead*. As I watched, a middle-aged lady at the back of the group dropped her pants, squatted, and relieved herself right there in the middle of the road! And then she hurried to catch up, fearful of being left behind. Exile.

Friends, I like my easy first world existence. Electricity, indoor plumbing, fast food, air conditioning. I *LIKE* it. But there may come a day when God calls some of us into exile. Cut off from the sheepfold. In the wind. I pray that if that day comes for us, that our heart's response will be that of the prophet Habakkuk, who not only rejoiced in his relationship with God in the midst of the trouble, but he *wrote songs about it.*

> *Yet I will rejoice in the LORD,*
> *I will be joyful in God my Savior.*
>
> *The Sovereign LORD is my strength.*
> *He makes my feet like the feet of a deer, he*
> *enables me to go on the heights.*

64.   Naked and Barefoot

Anyone else notice that in Isaiah 20, quoted from the *NIV*, God tells his prophet to take his clothes and shoes off, and go around naked and barefoot? And so he does. Did he ask, like I often do, "Was that really You, God?" Because... *that CAN'T be right!* Or did he know God so intimately that he knew it was God talking, and obeyed right away?

(What did his wife say?) Oh, and then the next verse casually mentions that it was for three years...

> *Then God said, "Just as my servant Isaiah has*
> *walked around town naked and barefooted for*
> *three years as a warning sign to Egypt and*

Ethiopia, so the king of Assyria is going to
come and take the Egyptians as captives and
the Ethiopians as exiles. He'll take young and
old alike and march them out of there naked
and barefooted, exposed to mockery and jeers –
the bared buttocks of Egypt on parade!
Everyone who has put hope in Ethiopia and
expected help from Egypt will be thrown into
confusion. Everyone who lives on this coast
will say, 'Look at them! Naked and barefooted,
shuffling off to exile! And we thought they were
our best hope, that they'd rescue us from the
king of Assyria. Now what's going to happen to
us? How are we going to get out of this?' "

Um... I have questions?

Did God say anything *else* to Isaiah during the three years of nakedness, discomfort, and shame? Or did Isaiah just plod along on the path God directed until God directed otherwise? Do I have that kind of patience? *Do I have that kind of relationship with God?* Not hardly.

This says Isaiah was a warning sign to Egypt and Ethiopia about the doom that was just over the horizon. Were there God-fearers in Egypt and Ethiopia who took notice? There are other examples in scripture of God warning pagan kings of pending disaster. Such as warning Pharaoh of a great famine, or Nebuchadnezzar of the world kingdoms to follow, or Belshazzar of the imminent end of his reign. (Incidentally, if God chose to warn pagan kings of disaster to come, why would we think He wouldn't talk to his own kids about his plans?)

117

Did God set up this whole situation so that His people Israel would be forced to rely on Him for protection, instead of others? What lengths will God go to in order for me to utterly rely on Him? And how can I be that close to God, where I recognize His voice, and obey without question, no matter the personal consequences?

Much to think about.

65.   Tickets to Disney

Those who know me well are probably aware that I stress a lot. I can get myself worked up over practically anything in under five minutes. (It's a *gift!*)

But tonight I am at peace. God grabbed me with a couple of scripture passages today. I opened this morning to Jeremiah 29. It's a popular passage of comfort. "For I know the plans I have for you," etc. But it is given to the exiles who had *JUST ARRIVED* in Babylon. They wanted to go home. But instead, God told them to settle down because they were going to be there for a minute. He told them to build houses, plant vineyards, get married, have kids, marry their kids off, and so forth. "And pray for the prosperity of the land, for as it prospers, so you too will prosper." Only then does God get around to emphasizing the long-term nature of their temporary situation. (As if telling them to plant vineyards, get married, have kids, and have grandkids wasn't enough of a clue.) I especially like how *The Message* puts it:

> *This is GOD's word on the subject: "As soon as Babylon's seventy years are up AND NOT A*

*DAY BEFORE, I'll show up and take care of
you as I promised and bring you back home. I
know what I'm doing. I have it all planned out –
plans to take care of you, not abandon you,
plans to give you the future you hope for.*

And then it gets to the REALLY good part!

*When you call on me, when you come and pray
to me, I'll listen. When you come looking for
me, you'll find me. Yes, when you get serious
about finding me and want it more than
anything else, I'll make sure you won't be
disappointed.*

GOD's Decree.

Could it be that God put them in exile to BLESS them and give
them a hunger for Him?

In my life I have some favorite things to worry about. My mind
habitually goes to these problems, and I turn them over and over
incessantly in my mind. But today as I did so, thoughtlessly
even, God impressed on me that this was not a real problem. It
was taken care of, and I didn't need to waste brain cells
worrying about it. In fact, continually fretting about it was a
slander against God's character, because it demonstrated a lack
of trust in God's goodness to me!

I had been acting like a little kid whose father had promised to
take him to Disney World that summer. First the kid got excited,
and then he got all whiney and clingy. *"Please Dad, PLEASE -
PLEASE - PLEASE - PLEASE take us to Disney!"* But, the
reality is, the issue was already settled. The tickets were already
purchased. The motel was reserved and paid for. They were

going to Disney this summer! Except... It's still April. So take a chill pill and go annoy your sister or something!

Then God quoted Daniel 12:13 in *The Message* to me, the final verse in the book of Daniel. He had just seen a horrible vision of the end times-- "The Worst Trouble the World Has Ever Seen", and he was understandably stressed. But here is what God told him:

> *And you? Go about your business without fretting or worrying. Relax. When it's all over, you will be on your feet to receive your reward.*

"So chill," God says, "I've got this."

66.   Believe Already!

I feel someone here is struggling with something God has told them. And the Enemy, like the serpent in the Garden of Eden, is whispering in their ear, *"Has God REALLY said...?"* This passage, Luke 1:18-20 *(MSG)*, is for you:

> *Zechariah said to the angel, "Do you expect me to believe this? I'm an old man and my wife is an old woman."*
> *But the angel said [in consternation], "I am Gabriel, the sentinel of God, sent especially to bring you this glad news. But because you won't believe me, you'll be unable to say a word until the day of your son's birth. Every word I've spoken to you will come true on time – GOD'S time."*

So BELIEVE already!

67. When Two Full Years Had Passed...

This morning I was journaling and was asking God about timing. Then I looked up and my eyes fell on Genesis 41:1 in the *NIV:*

> *When two full years had passed, Pharaoh had a dream...*

The back story? Joseph was a prisoner. Falsely accused of attempted rape by his boss' wife. It was just the latest in a series of injustices. Back when he was 17, God gave him two dreams about being in charge, and his family bowing down to him. Understandably, it didn't go over well at the dinner table when he shared those little tidbits. His brothers sold him into slavery soon after and faked his death. He was purchased by Potiphar, and then became the first man on earth imprisoned for *NOT* having sex with a willing woman!

The bible is vague about the time frame, but *sometime later,* Pharaoh's chief baker and chief cupbearer (the royal taste-tester) offended the big boss and got thrown in prison.

> *After they had been in custody for some time, each of the two men – the cupbearer and the baker of the king of Egypt, who were being held in prison - had a dream the same night, and each dream had a meaning of its own.*

Joseph successfully interprets the dreams, and they both come to pass. The baker is executed, and the cupbearer is restored to his position. Now it's time for him to return the favor to Joseph, whisper in Pharaoh's ear, and spring Joseph from the joint! But sadly, no.

When two full years had passed, Pharaoh had a dream...

The cupbearer (in Pharaoh's intimate confidence as his poison insurance) finally remembers and introduces Joseph. Pharaoh's dream is interpreted, and Joseph is made prime minister. He then proceeds to save the world. Cool! Just like in the movies!

Except Genesis 41:46 notes that Joseph was 30 years old when he entered Pharaoh's service. So, 12-13 years of exile, slavery, and prison. And then another seven years of hard work before he saw his family and they bowed to him – twenty years after God gave him the dreams. Why?

Because God had stuff to do IN Joseph before he would be truly useful. That sort of thing takes time. And often, suffering.

There is a great song by Vertical Worship called *Yes I Will*.

> *I count on one thing*
> *The same God that never fails*
> *Will not fail me now*
> *You won't fail me now*
> *In the waiting*
> *The same God who's never late*
> *Is working all things out*
> *You're working all things out.*[20]

---

[20] Eddie Hoagland, Jonathan Smith, Mia Fieldes, *Yes I Will,* album Bright Faith Bold Future, 2018, track 2, produced by Jonathan Smith, Provident Music Group, Franklin TN, https://www.youtube.com/watch?v=NrTv39-lG4M

So if you're *"In The Waiting,"* then *TRUST* that God will work it out, even if it takes years. Meanwhile, be *PRESENT*. This day, *TODAY*, is the critical moment.

Walk with God today and trust Him with tomorrow.

68.   The Cliff Edge of Doom

For the past week or so, God has been showing me a ship in a storm, with huge waves, torn sails, spars in disarray, a severe roll, and perhaps a broken mast – much like the 1680 painting of a 70-gun British man-of-war caught in a violent squall, by Willem van de Velde.

I cried at work today. It had been a while, so I guess I was due. A major piece of equipment broke, and the problem seemed insurmountable. It still does. It's overwhelming.

But tonight I read a familiar passage in a new way. It was Psalms 46:1-3. Most of us are probably familiar with *The New International Version's* telling:

> *God is our refuge and strength,*
> *an ever-present help in trouble.*
> *Therefore we will not fear, though the earth give way*
> *and the mountains fall into the heart of the sea,*
> *though its waters roar and foam*
> *and the mountains quake with their surging.*

This is nice, but for me it's like watching a National Geographic Special on volcanoes in Hawaii and seeing hot lava flow into the ocean. There is steam everywhere, but this is entertainment rather than personal risk. The language of *The Message* however, makes it more immediate-- more personal:

> *God is a safe place to hide,*
> *ready to help when we need him.*
> *We stand fearless at the cliff-edge of doom,*
> *courageous in seastorm and earthquake,*
> *Before the rush and roar of oceans,*
> *the tremors that shift mountains...*

"God is a safe place to hide." For me, that's evocative not just of shelter in a storm, but concealment from the hunter. "We stand fearless at the cliff-edge of doom, courageous in seastorm and earthquake." Our peril is real. It is immediate. We are standing at the edge, and it is crumbling under our feet. Imminent peril. But God is present and available to cling to.

I work on the water, and once lived down the road from where Herman Melville penned his novel Moby Dick. I love the sea and ships, and sailing. And yet... I have a tremendous fear of drowning. Such that swimming in open water gives me an anxiety attack. Yet, I am a dock builder. Go figure. For me, a big storm at sea in a sailing ship would be my own personal worst nightmare. Utterly terrifying. "We stand courageous in seastorm and earthquake."

I am reminded of John 12:27-28, in *The Message*, where Jesus is laying it all out for his disciples:

> *Right now I am storm-tossed. And what am I*
> *going to say? "Father, get me out of this"? No,*
> *this is why I came in the first place. I'll say,*
> *"Father, put your glory on display."*

So my friends, if you are storm-tossed right now and need prayer or just someone to listen, I'm available. And please pray for me too!

"Father, put your glory on display."

69. The Good Story

I am enjoying *The First Nations Version: An Indigenous translation of the New Testament",* published by Intervarsity Press.[21]

> *"This translation of the good story is dedicated to the Indigenous Peoples of Turtle Island (North America)- the Tribal Nations that call this land home. We pray the First Nations Version will bring healing to those who have suffered under the dominance of colonial governments who, with the help of churches and missionary organizations, often took our land, our languages, our culture, and even our children. As our Tribal Nations work hard to reclaim what has been stolen, it is our hope that the colonial language that was forced upon us can now serve our people in a good way, by presenting Creator Sets Free (Jesus) in a more culturally relevant context."*

[21] Terry M. Wildman, *First Nations Version: An Indigenous Translation of the New Testament* (Westmont, IL: InterVarsity Press, 2021), vi, 450-451, vii-viii.

Here is an excerpt, from Revelation 3:7-13

> *Write this to the messenger of the sacred family that gathers in the village of the Family of Friends (Philadelphia):*
>
> *These are the words of the holy and true One, the one who has the rightful power of Much Loved One (David.) When he opens the way, no one can close it, and when he closes the way, no one else can open it.*
>
> *This is what the holy and true one has to say: I know what you have been doing. Behold! I have opened a way before you that no one can block. Even though your strength is small, you have stayed true to my message and have not turned away from representing me. Look what I will do to the members of the gathering house of the Accuser (Satan) who falsely represent themselves as true-hearted Tribal Members. I will cause them to humble themselves before you to honor you. I will make sure they clearly see that I have loved you.*
>
> *Because you have walked with firm steps and stayed true to my message, I will watch over you and keep you safe from the time of great trouble that is coming upon the world, to test the ones that walk the land. It will not be long, for I am coming soon. Hold on to what you already have with a strong hand. Then no one will be able to take your headdress of honor away from you.*

*To the ones who win the victory I will make
them a strong pole in the sacred lodge of my
Father the Great Spirit – and there they will
remain. I will carve into them the name of my
Father the Great Spirit and the name of his
sacred village that comes down from the world
above – the new Village of Peace (Jerusalem). I
will also carve into them my own new name.
Let the one who has ears hear and do what the
Spirit is saying to the sacred families.*

I particularly enjoy the names the translators use. They put the standard English names in parenthesis in the text. Some of my favorite personal names include:

- *Bitter Tears (Mary)*

- *He Gives Sons (Joseph)*

- *Creator Will Remember (Zechariah)*

- *Creator Is My Promise (Elizabeth)*

- *Gift of Goodwill (John the Baptist)*

- *He Made Us Laugh (Isaac)*

- *Heel Grabber (Jacob)*

- *Small Man (Paul)*

Also, the names of the books of the New Testament in this translation are full of meaning:

- *Gift from Creator Tells the Good Story (Matthew)*

- *War Club tells the Good Story (Mark)*

- *Shining Light tells the Good Story (Luke)*

127

- *He Shows Goodwill tells the Good Story (John)*

- *The Good Story Continues (Acts)*

- *Small Man to the Sacred Family in the Village of Iron (Romans)*

- *First and Second Letter from Small Man to the Sacred Family in the Village of Pleasure (Corinthians)*

- *Small Man to the Sacred Family in the land of Pale Skins (Galatians)*

- *Small Man to the Sacred Family in the Village of Desire (Ephesians)*

- *Small Man to the Sacred Family in the Village of Horses (Philippians)*

- *Small Man to the Sacred Family in the Village of Giants (Colossians)*

- *First and Second letters from Small Man to the Sacred Family in Village of False Victory (Thessalonians)*

- *First and Second letters from Small Man to He Gives Honor (Timothy)*

- *Small Man to Big Man (Titus)*

- *Small Man to He Shows Kindness (Philemon)*

- *To the People of the Tribes of Wrestles with Creator (Hebrews)*

- *He Leads the Way to the Scattered Tribes (James)*

- *First, Second, and Third Letters from Stands on the Rock (Peter)*
- *First, Second, and Third Letters from He Shows Goodwill (John)*
- *Strong of Heart (Jude)*
- *Book of the Great Revealing (Revelation)* [22]

May we each see things with new eyes today, and may we tell the Good Story!

70.   The - God - Who - Sees - Me

I like interesting names. My son and I enjoy listening to the *Expeditionary Force* series of Sci-Fi novels by Craig Alanson on Audible, about a crew of space-faring humans, who are traveling the galaxy with an alien Artificial Intelligence in the shape of a beer can. (Yes, really.) During their adventures, they encounter multiple alien species that have been warring so long that they have run out of warship names and started hyphenating them. My favorite is the battleship sporting the name *I - Am - Itching - To - Give - Someone - A - Beat-down - And - Today - Is - Your - Lucky - Day.* Interesting names are great! In fact, I once had a crush on a beautiful Colombian girl named "Cielo"- Spanish for "Heaven." (I mean, who *wouldn't* want to go home each night to heaven?)

---

[22] Terry M. Wildman, *First Nations Version: An Indigenous Translation of the New Testament* (Westmont, IL: InterVarsity Press, 2021), vi, 450-451, vii-viii.

Sometimes we pick out names for God ourselves, based on our own encounters with Him. Pregnant slave girl Hagar, running away from her mistress while carrying her master's baby, encountered God as she stopped for water (Genesis 16). God told her to go back home. And then told her about the future of her unborn son, and of descendants too numerous to count. In response, she named Him **"The - God - Who - Sees - Me."** Isn't that what we all want – *to be seen?*

The Indigenous Peoples New Testament chose "Bitter Tears" as the name for Mary, the mother of Jesus. I wonder, *did Mary cry Bitter Tears because she felt unseen?* Misunderstood? Unseen that is, until she was pregnant out of wedlock, and not by her fiancé? And suddenly she felt *EVERYONE's* eyes on her?

My own preferred name for God is **"The - God - Whose - Timing - Is - Perfect."** And he reminds me of that name from time to time when I need it. Tonight I encountered a cool one in Joel 2:26, in *The Message.* "You'll be full of praises to your GOD, **'The - God - Who - Has - Set - You - Back - On - Your - Heels - In - Wonder.'** " That's awesome!

So here's a challenge. Has God ever set you back on your heels in wonder as you encountered Him? Care to share? I would love to hear about your experience!

71. Teasing

A bit about me... I grew up in a household where teasing = affection. (Thanks Dad.) I *ONLY* tease people I feel close to. People I feel very comfortable with. So if I am pushing your buttons, you are *IN* with me. A synonym expression would be "yanking your chain", but I only use that expression with men, because I worry about women getting upset about the dog imagery. *"Are you calling me a dog?!?!")* In contrast, if I am formal with you, we are *NOT* close. (Also, if we *ARE* close, I bombard you with memes. Apparently it's my love language. #sorrynotsorry.)

I have a teenage daughter who amazes me with her interests and abilities and who is very unlike me in her chaos tolerance in places like the kitchen. She's a teensy bit OCD. All the dishes *MUST* be stacked by shape and color. I like pushing her buttons -- messing with her -- by mismatching the stacks of bowls and the Blue Bell ice cream lids. I think of it, not as being mean, but as teaching her to cope when life is messy. Life is *NOT* always decent and in order. Life (and love—*ESPECIALLY LOVE*), gets messy.

She is getting a lot better about this now, but when she was younger, she would exasperate me when I wanted to take her on a daddy-daughter date, by demanding to know every blessed detail, and by trying to negotiate the timing of our departure. She had to wash her hair, and do homework, or something else today, and demanded to know *SPECIFICALLY* where we were going, how long we would be at each stop, what we would do there, and when we would get back home. She wanted to get all the details straight in her mind before agreeing to go. I just wanted her to trust me, and to get in the car. We were going to the animal shelter to play with the kitties, to a coffee shop, and to Hobby Lobby to buy jewelry-making supplies. She was going to have the best time! Because I really do have her best interest at heart, and I *DELIGHT* in giving her nice surprises. So get in the car already!

We want to know details. To be in control. Except, life doesn't work that way. God's kingdom doesn't work that way. The disciples were asking Jesus about the timing for the end of the age. *"You don't get to know the timing,"* he told them. *"Timing is the Father's business."* In Matthew 16:24-25 *(MSG)*, he told them,

> *Anyone who intends to come with me has to let me lead. You're not in the driver's seat; I am. Don't run from suffering; embrace it. Follow me and I'll show you how.*

So yesterday, I was stressing to God about stuff, and asking Him for details. In response, He spoke to my heart and said, *"You're just going to have to trust me."* He was taking me back to the daddy-daughter date scenario. I was trying to plan it all out *MYSELF*, but He was really saying,

> *"I love you and have your best interest at heart. So just get in the car."*

I wept.

72. Quote of the Day

Question: "How did you become a Christian?"

Answer: "The person I was beating wouldn't stop talking about Jesus."

(From a conversation recalled by a missionary friend discussing a recent visit to Ethiopia.)

73. The Oblivious Diners and the Block E.

Where to start? Years ago, when we were young and dumb, my friends James and Angie and I decided to take a midnight drive to Galveston, Texas, to the Admiral Hotel and their big concrete fishing pier, just to watch the huge waves roll in from a distant hurricane. They were impressive, passing just under the massive concrete frame of the pier. We enjoyed the spectacle and went on our merry way. But later that night, those waves destroyed that pier.

So last night, I had a dream. In the dream, I was at a nice restaurant by the water. The 2nd floor room was filled to capacity and a storm was raging outside. Enormous waves were crashing against shore, and some of them came up as high as the windows of the dining room and splashed against the glass of the big picture windows-- much like water splashing against the bridge of a ship at sea from a sudden rogue wave. Alarming! Except nobody was alarmed. They enjoyed the excitement of the waves, but went back to eating their dinner, oblivious to their danger.

About a week ago, God showed me something else strange. I was looking at a map of the United States. As I watched, the states started moving. They started sliding, stretching, and compressing to form a capital (uppercase) letter "E." I started asking God what it meant. What did the E stand for? Energy? Emmanuel? Mid-term Elections? While I was thinking about it, two passages came to mind. One was Isaiah 8:6-8, quoted from *The New International Version:*

*Because this people has rejected the gently
flowing waters of Shiloh and rejoices over
Rezin and the son of Remaliah, therefore the
Lord is about to bring against them the mighty
floodwaters of the River-- the king of Assyria
with all his pomp. It will overflow all its
channels, run over all its banks and sweep into
Judah, swirling over it, passing through it and
reaching up to the neck. It's outspread wings
will cover the breadth of your land, oh
Emmanuel!*

The other passage was Isaiah 9:1-2 in the *NIV*, a beautiful Messianic passage:

*Nevertheless, there will be no more gloom for
those who were in distress. In the past He
humbled the land of Zebulon and the land of
Naphtali, but in the future He will honor
Galilee of the Gentiles, by the way of the sea,
along the Jordan.*

*The people walking in darkness have seen a
great light; on those living in the land of the
shadow of death a light has dawned.*

Here's what I think. The dream of the dining room and the Capital E are linked, much like Pharaoh's dream of the fat and skinny ears of corn, followed by a dream of fat and skinny cows were linked. The Ukraine war (and upcoming Taiwan war) are for the moment, just entertainment. Other people's problems. *(This food is really delicious, isn't it?)* But soon the windows will break, the sea will pour in, and the destruction of war will flood our land.

But God...

But God wants to use this to turn our hearts towards Him. I think the Isaiah 9:1-2 passage interprets it, "The people walking in darkness have seen a great light." In response, the nation will align themselves with him, showing their affinity in the shape of the letter E. Much like the 300 member fightin' Texas Aggie Band forms a Block "T" (for Texas A&M) when they march at football games.

But maybe I am all wrong. Maybe the block "E" vision was totally about the mid-term election, and about States aligning themselves. Maybe it means something else entirely. But this is what I saw. Pray about it. Ask God for yourselves what it means. If this resonates with you, great. If not, I tried. Thanks for listening.

God's peace be upon you. Peace in the midst of the storm.

74.   A Song for the Frazzled

I wrote this on Thanksgiving 2020. *A Song for the Frazzled (Mommies and Daddies.)* If you have young kids, let me say *You Can Do This!* And don't be afraid to ask your friends and family for help.

Blessings!

> *Little girls, wanting to be held*
> *Little boys, saying "watch me run!"*
> *They need love – can't you tell?*
> *Give them time. Give them time.*
>
> *Father love wash over me,*
> *Open up my eyes.*
> *Give me grace to pass along*
> *As you give me time.*
> *Little girls, jumping on my bed*
> *Leaping dancing laughing boys*
> *Stinky diapers, random mess.*
> *Children are a joy!*
>
> *Father love wash over me,*
> *Open up my eyes.*
> *Give me grace to pass along,*
> *As you give me time.*
>
> *Little girls, wanting to be held*
> *Little boys, saying watch me run*
> *They need love – can't you tell?*
> *Give them time, give them time.*

75. Alone-ness

God has been speaking to me lately about "alone-ness," and about being fearful. (And perhaps, deep inside, about being fearful of loneliness?)

Years ago, we had a 3" snowfall in southwest Virginia (big deal), and the boys had spent the night with their grandparents to go sledding. So in the morning, my totally altruistic daughter came to me with a proposal:

> *Daddy, can you take me to Boompa and*
> *Granna Bear's, so you and Mommy can have*
> *Alone-ness?*

Uh-huh. But as my sister-in-law pointed out, you have got to respect the hustle.

We hear about God taking us to "The Wilderness" and inwardly cringe. We think about Moses on the backside of the desert. For 40 years... And of the children of Israel wandering in the wilderness for 40 years, *UNTIL THEY DIED*. And of Paul spending two years in the desert in Arabia after his conversion, during which time we hear *NOTHING* from him. ("But what about his Ministry?")

But really, we have it all wrong. The wilderness isn't about God taking us to the woodshed for punishment. It's about intimacy. Alone-ness. Matthew 4:1-2 in *The Message* tells us,

> *Next, Jesus was taken into the wild by the Spirit*
> *for the Test. The Devil was ready to give it.*
> *Jesus prepared for the Test by fasting forty*
> *days and forty nights...*

In the wilderness... That's where God prepared him for "The Test." But going to the wilderness was a regular practice for Jesus. Matthew 14:22-23 in *The New International Version* tells us:

> *As soon as the meal was finished, he insisted that the disciples get in the boat and go on ahead to the other side while he dismissed the people...*

What meal? The feeding of the five thousand!

> *With the crowd dispersed, he climbed the mountain so that he could be by himself to pray. He stayed there alone, late into the night.*

So let me get this straight. He was doing *MINISTRY*. Huge crowds were gathering, and God was doing *MIRACLES!* Yet Jesus shut it all down and went away to pray. By himself. Because *He NEEDED Alone-ness with Father God.*

In Lamentations 3:2 in *The Message*, a passage God has used personally to rock my world over and over, Jeremiah writes:

> *He took me by the hand and walked me into pitch black darkness.*

Oh wow. Not my favorite passage. No sir. But that's what God did with me. He took me by the hand and led me into the pitch-black darkness of the COVID forest and ten days in the hospital. And then he led me out. That was a wilderness experience for me. No human contact except for the doctors and nurses in protective gear, head to toe: scrubs, booties, aprons, gloves, double masks, goggles, *AND* face plates. But I was grateful for their brief presence. Sometimes God puts us in hard situations.

At least four of my friends are grieving lost spouses or parents right now. Pain, pain, and more pain. But here they are.

In Exodus 3-4, Moses encounters God at the burning bush. It starts out well, but then God gives him a mission. It's a tough one, and he balks. In response God gives him a *TEST,* right then and there. (**Pro Tip:** tread lightly with the mission objections when dealing with Sovereign God.)

God:	What is in your hand?
Moses:.	A staff
God:.	Throw it on the ground.

Moses does, and it becomes a poisonous snake. Moses jumps back – fast!

God:.	Reach out and grab it by the tail.
Moses:	Wait! What?!?!

Moses grabs it by the tail, and it turns back into a staff. Personally? I *LOATHE* and fear snakes. All kinds and sizes. For me, this would be a horrid test. But Moses did it. He passed the test, in spite of his fear.

As I write this, some of you are in the wilderness of loneliness. And others are about to be. I pray that it will be transformed for you from loneliness to alone-ness with the living God.

Grab it by the tail.

76. Twice Saved

I woke up early, to a gorgeous sunrise – the sky orange outside my window. I went to the kitchen for my coffee and opened at random to this passage. It is Psalm 65:1-8, quoted from *The Message*, and is the perfect passage for this glorious morning.

> *Silence is praise to you, Zion-dwelling God,*
> *And also obedience. You hear the*
> *prayer in it all.*
>
> *We all arrive at your doorstep sooner or later,*
> *loaded with guilt,*
> *Our sins are too much for us—*
> *but you get rid of them once and for all.*
> *Blessed are the chosen!*
> *Blessed the guest at home in your place!*
> *We expect our fill of good things in your house,*
> *your heavenly manse.*
> *All your salvation wonders*
> *are on display in your trophy room.*
> *Earth-Tamer, Ocean-Pourer,*
> *Mountain-Maker, Hill-Dresser,*
> *Muzzler of sea storm and wave crash,*
> *of mobs in noisy riot—*
> *far and wide they'll come to a stop,*
> *they'll stare in wonder.*
> *Dawn and dusk take turns calling,*
> *"Come and worship."*

A sweetly poetic passage, but it evokes powerful memories for me.

Muzzler of sea storm and wave crash, of mobs
in noisy riot...

Many years ago, I was working in a predominantly Muslim country in the former Soviet Union. While I was there, I was part of a local church body, and the church was having special meetings. A group of us were passing out flyers inviting people to come to these meetings to hear what God says will happen in the future, and we were having good discussions with people.

It was going great – until it wasn't. The crowd turned ugly, and I was attacked by the guards from the nearby Iranian embassy. They were in the process of kidnapping me – physically dragging me off to their embassy – when they suddenly let go and ran away. I looked up from the ground at a burly policeman leaning over me. The crowd had melted away, and he said simply *"you may go."* I got out of there, rejoined my group at a friend's apartment, and had a total breakdown-- asthma, tears, the works. But I was uninjured. A few days later, my friend Leah was confronted by that same policeman. *"I am your savior,"* he said.

Come again?

> *I am the man who rescued you. I am the*
> *policeman in charge of this district, and so I*
> *have to know what you're doing here.*

"YES!!!" she replied. "YOU are the policeman in charge of our district, and you HAVE to know what we're doing here. It's your JOB!" [stamps foot for emphasis.] *"And now YOU and EVERY ONE OF YOUR MEN MUST GO TO THESE MEETINGS."*

The chutzpah of this woman! I don't know if the police ever came or not, but this changed my whole perspective on holy boldness. So thanks Leah.

> *Muzzler of sea storm and wave crash,*
> *of mobs in noisy riot.*

And thank you God, for sending me *TWO* saviors. One of them two millennia ago, at Christmas, and another in the form of an important policeman with his walrus mustache.

Twice saved!

77. My Homegirl Ruth

I'm thinking about my homegirl Ruth this morning. We probably all know the story. She meets a great guy, gets married, and spends 10 years in wedded bliss, and then he up and dies on her. (The nerve!) As does her father-in-law *AND* her brother-in-law. Disaster upon disaster. And so unfair! *WHY*, God? Why *ME?* The unanswerable question. Unbearable sorrow.

She chooses to travel with her mother-in-law back to the land of Judah. A strange country, where she has nothing and knows nobody. But God already made provision for her. Her Boaz was waiting.

Cool story bro. Yeah, we know this part. He meets her, loves her, marries her, and they have kids together. Her great grandson ends up being King David. But what we tend to miss here is that not only was she a foreigner, but she was also from

Moab – so *she was black-listed BY LAW from **EVER** being one of God's people.* Deuteronomy 23:3-6 in *The Message* states:

> *No Ammonite or Moabite is to enter*
> *the congregation of GOD, even to the tenth*
> *generation, nor any of his children, ever. Those*
> *nations didn't treat you with hospitality on your*
> *travels out of Egypt, and on top of that, they*
> *hired Baalam son of Beor from Pethor in*
> *Mesopotamia to curse you. GOD, your God,*
> *refused to listen to Balaam but turned the curse*
> *into a blessing – how GOD your God loves*
> *you! Don't even try to get along with them, or*
> *do anything for them, EVER.*

So here she is – not just a foreigner, but an explicitly *prohibited* foreigner. (Others prohibited in this chapter from the assembly – the fellowship of believers – included Bastards and those with crushed or mutilated genitals.) Yet God had a plan for her – a big one.

I am reminded of Peter's vision in Acts 10 of the sheet being let down from heaven, filled with ritually unclean four-footed animals, reptiles, and birds. A voice told him, "Get up Peter, kill and eat." Peter argues with God, reminding God of the law against eating unclean animals. The voice spoke to him a second time. "Do not call anything impure that God has made clean." God was giving Peter, a devout Jew, a heads-up that Gentiles (shudder) were about to knock on his door. And he was to welcome them with open arms.

So maybe someone reading this feels like an outsider, or unclean. Maybe your parents were married, but not to each other. Maybe you had an abortion. Or maybe you had a baby when you weren't married. Maybe you have trashed your body with drugs or alcohol. Maybe you've committed crimes and done time. Or cheated on your spouse. Or are covered with tattoos and piercings. Or have multiple sex partners. Or are in a same-sex relationship. Maybe you have had sex change surgery. Maybe you're addicted to pornography and visiting hookers. (Insert impossible situation here _____.) For whatever reason, you feel you are on God's blacklist. But maybe now it's time to come home?

> *Do not call anything impure that God has made clean.*

Start fresh with God. Just come home.

78. The Driver

Last night, I dreamed I was riding as a passenger in a big semi. We were in heavy traffic with lots of stop lights and sharp turns. Idiot car drivers were cutting us off and risking their lives trying to pass us on the inside of our turns to gain 5 seconds of advantage. (This is my personal nightmare when driving my own truck and trailer, and it's an easy-to-drive automatic.)

In the dream, the gear shift wasn't three-stick like in some of the cool older trucks I have seen, but the shift pattern seemed equally complicated. I love driving little 6-speed stick-shift convertibles, but I didn't have a prayer of driving this monster. But this driver was *GOOD*, floating the gears, picking just the right time to shift, and never missing the gear he needed. No grinding, just sweet perfection. I had to respect the awesomeness.

I noticed that the trip was taking a long time, and then we were in the mountains. Steep upgrades and downgrades, with runaway truck ramps flashing by. But my driver never broke a sweat. I was *SO THANKFUL* it wasn't me driving. While I was thinking about the dream, Matthew 16:24-25 in *The Message* came to mind:

> *Then Jesus went to work on his disciples.*
>
> *"Anyone who intends to come after me has to let me lead.*
> *You're not in the driver's seat; I am..."*

I tend to be destination-oriented. I am always thinking about the next milestone, the next checkbox, the next check coming in, the next big sale, the pie-in-the-sky future I am striving for. I'm the little kid who drives his father crazy on the big family road trip to California by asking every 15 minutes, *"Are we almost there???"* But really, this is a lifelong road trip, with new experiences at every mile. The process is the product. So buckle up and enjoy watching the skill of the Master as he works the gears.

I also think about what a control freak I am about driving. I would much rather be the driver because other people just scare me. Sometimes as a passenger, I have to close my eyes or read a book, just to keep my anxiety down. But this is more like a standard scene out of a James Bond or Jason Bourne movie, where the hero comes to the driver's door and says, *"Move over, I'm driving."* This is followed by a massive car chase, with helicopters, motorcycles, machine guns, etc. The car owner had no chance of surviving what was coming. Not as the driver. But releasing control changed everything.

"Move over," God says. "I'm driving."

79.   Connection

I like names. Especially descriptive names. I think modern English language names suck, because their meaning is usually lost to us unless we look them up in a baby book. They *HAVE* meaning, to be sure. But for us, they usually serve only as identification of the individual, or a tribute to someone from the past that we admire. They are not a character reference or a reminder of heroic acts, unlike the Bible names or the native American names of our past. Even the fictitious ones are cool. I'm thinking of *Stands - With - A - Fist* and *Dances - With - Wolves*, from the Kevin Costner movie by that name.

In the Bible, people often named their children for what they hoped or expected them to do. In Isaiah 7:14, God told king Ahaz through the prophet Isaiah that the future Messiah would be named Immanuel, **God - With - Us.** Not God-Far-Off. Not God-Who-Doesn't-Care, but God *-WITH* - Us. *GOD - PRESENT - IN - OUR - SUFFERING.*

Sometimes, people named their children based on what was going on in their own lives; on God's dealings with them. In I Samuel 1:20, Hannah names her baby son Samuel *"because I asked God for him."*

In Genesis 29, Jacob meets Rachel and falls in love at first sight. So much so that he kisses her *FIRST*, and only *THEN* introduces himself. (Look it up.) He offers her father seven years of free labor in exchange for her hand in marriage, but after all those years of work her father swindles him and marries his oldest daughter Leah to him instead. What the what?!?! The morning after, Laban offers the irate Jacob a new deal. Work another seven years, and he can have Rachel too.

Jacob agreed. When he'd completed the honeymoon week, Laban gave him his daughter Rachel to be his wife. (Laban gave his maid Bilhah to his daughter Rachel as her maid.) Jacob then slept with her. And he loved Rachel more than Leah. He worked for Laban another seven years.

When God realized that Leah was unloved, he opened her womb. But Rachel was barren. Leah became pregnant and had a son. She named him Reuben (Look - It's - A - Boy!). "This is a sign," she said, "that God has seen my misery; and a sign that now my husband will love me."

She became pregnant again and had another son. "God heard," she said, "that I was unloved and so he gave me this son also." She named this one Simeon (God - Heard).

She became pregnant yet again – another son. She said, now maybe my husband will connect with me-- I've given him three sons!" That's why she named him Levi (Connect).

She became pregnant a final time and had a fourth son. She said, "This time I'll praise

> *GOD." So she named him Judah (Praise -*
> *God). Then she stopped having children.*
> *-Genesis 29:28-35, The Message*

I think it's fascinating that it says God noticed that Leah was unloved, and so he opened her womb. God cares about the love - the connection between husbands and wives. Even (especially?) in arranged marriages. Ephesians 5:28-29 *(NIV)* instructs husbands to love their wives, just as Christ loved the church and gave himself up for her...

> *In this same way, husbands ought to love their*
> *wives as their own bodies. He who loves his*
> *wife loves himself. After all, no one ever hated*
> *his own body, but he feeds and cares for it, just*
> *as Christ does the church.*

Did you notice that the name of Leah's third son means "Connection"? Another translation phrases it, "Now at last my husband will become attached to me because I have born him three sons." God cares so much about this connection between spouses that-- **WATCH THIS!** -- God chose the tribe of Levi, whose name means **CONNECTION,** to be the priestly tribe... The tribe that ministered as priests in the temple -- the *connection* between God and the rest of the people. Because God is all about intimacy. That's what this Christian life is all about. A love relationship with God. Intimacy. Connection.

As we go about our lives this week, may God strengthen our connection, our intimacy, with himself and with our spouses. And may He show us what needs to change to strengthen those connections.

So go connect!

80.　Happy Anniversary to ME!

One year ago today, I was admitted to the hospital with COVID, and was Released to Life 11 days later. God is good. It's been a hard year at times, especially during the first few weeks and months. But I thank you, my friends, for sharing the journey with me. And for encouraging my attempt at writing here on Facebook, which started from my hospital bed. I never once thought of myself as a writer. But someday, perhaps...

Blessings, and my most sincere thanks.

81.　Fish Tea and Fellowship

Have you ever had "Fish Tea"? I have! Years ago I was on a business trip in Azerbaijan with my boss. We were in a small provincial town and were in a meeting with a local business leader. This guy had his fingers in everything in town. The furniture factory, the car dealership, the fish hatchery, hazelnuts... I think he ran the place. And he was oily. We couldn't wait to get out of there. As the time came for the meeting to end, he came out with the traditional *"Come to my house for dinner."* This was normal there, especially when meeting foreigners. It is like an American saying, *"Hi, how are you?"* It's a nicety. They don't mean it, so don't start blabbing your life story. So in Azerbaijan, you absolutely MUST refuse at least three times. (They could feel culturally obligated to blow a month's wages on having you to dinner, so don't you dare!)

149

Anyway, we had dinner waiting down the road with our host family, but this guy wasn't hearing it. After our many protests, it became *"Come to my house for Tea."* *"Um, okay,"* my boss said. *"We can do that."* What my boss didn't realize was that there was a samovar in the next room, and tea could have (and should have!) been served with a snap of his fingers. So off we go.

We get to this man's farm, and he disappears, leaving us with one of his associates for the farm tour and an extended lecture on hazelnut fertilization, harvesting, marketing, export, and Azerbaijan's position on the world hazelnut commodities market. Interesting, yes, but this was taking forever! Eventually we were called into a banquet hall with place settings for 30 people and bread and fish on plates. *"I thought we were having tea?"* my boss asked. *"It's FISH Tea,"* was the answer.

Nonsense.

It was a set-up. He then proceeded to rump-butt the guy opposite us out of the way and to put kabob and fish on our plate personally. Because one of the highest honors you can do for someone there is to have them as a guest in your home and personally serve them a meal cooked by your own hands. We were now his guests. We were now under his protection, and WE were now culturally obligated to do him no harm. (What he was really worried about was us muscling in on his business interests, and this closed that door to us *AND* gave him local bragging rights.) So we had "Fish Tea" with all the trimmings with this dear man.

I'm a severe introvert. Lingering in fellowship isn't really my thing. But the Bible is *FULL* of it. Especially when meeting

150

with God. Notice how in Judges 6, when the angel of God wants to talk to Gideon, he comes to Gideon's jobsite and sits down under the tree while he was trying to work. ("Um, God, I'm a little busy here?") And when a stranger comes to your place and sits down (ugh), you KNOW they plan to stay awhile.

Angel: *"God is with you, O mighty warrior!"*

Gideon: *"With ME, my master?"* (You're kidding, right?)

"If God is with us, why has all this happened to us?"

They talk and Gideon asks for a sign that this is for real. That God *REALLY IS* going to deliver Israel through him. So here's the sign he asked for: *"DON'T GO* until I have made you dinner."

As a rabbit trail, some of us are so insecure that we *EXPECT* people to leave us. I spent my first several years of marriage begging my wife not to leave me. I thought that if she really got to know me-- who I really was deep inside -- that she would be out of there. She eventually loved this particular insecurity out of me, and I am grateful. So I wonder. Was Gideon being insecure? Was he worried the angel would change his mind about him, and pick someone else? Someone more ... suitable?

The angel agrees to wait, and Gideon rushes off. He slaughters, skins and butchers a goat, cooks it, bakes bread from scratch, and brings it to the angel as a sacred meal. Bread, broth, and meat. The angel touches the offering with his staff, it all bursts into flame and the angel ascends back to God in the flame. The angel had hung around as requested while the meal was being prepared, and I'll bet they talked the whole time.

In Genesis 18, it's the same thing. Hospitality. Three visitors appear to Abraham in the heat of the day. He washes their feet and orders a feast. A calf is butchered and cooked. Bread is made, and they eat together. But meal prep from mooing to meat takes *TIME*. No fridge, no microwave. I'll bet it took *HOURS*. And they were happy to linger. Abraham didn't offer them tea and then send them on their way. He gave them his time. He hung out with them, and in the process, the Lord told his 99 year-old host that his wife Sarah would have a son about this time next year. And then God gave Abraham a heads up, as his friend and confident, of what was about to go down in Sodom and Gomorrah. This may seem surprising that God would share something like that with Abraham, but Amos 3:7 tells us,

> *Surely the Sovereign LORD does nothing*
> *without revealing his plan to his*
> *servants the prophets.*

And so Abraham pleaded with God for mercy for the inhabitants. So *MUCH* important stuff was passed along to Abraham during this dinner together – this fellowship time.

And notice in Genesis 3:8 *(NIV)*, after Adam and Eve had eaten the forbidden fruit:

> *Then the man and his wife heard the sound of*
> *the LORD God as he was walking in the garden*
> *in the cool of the day, and they hid from the*
> *LORD God among the trees of the garden. But*
> *the LORD God called to the man, "Where are*
> *you?"*

Why this question? I would have thundered with a voice of many waters, *"WHAT HAVE YOU DONE!?!?"* (God would eventually get around to asking that terrible question.)

But God's first question was "Where are you?"-- because *God's heart was for FELLOWSHIP, not punishment.* Hanging out with God was the norm, *AND GOD MISSED HANGING OUT.* God would walk and talk with Adam and Eve in the garden in the cool of the evening. It was a regular thing. It was routine. Adam and Eve were supposed to be there, but they were hiding. God wasn't asking for a location check because He was confused. It was a rhetorical question. *God was calling them back to fellowship.* To the routine of talking with Him in the cool of the evening. Just like they did every night.

I think God enjoys it when we talk with him. When we just hang out and be real with Him. It will probably take a minute. So get alone with God and linger awhile. And then linger some more. Who knows what He might talk to you about?

> *Call to me, and I will answer you*
> *and tell you great and unsearchable things you*
> *do not know.*
> $\qquad$ *- Jeremiah 33:3, (NIV)*

153

82. Christmas Shave

This picture was taken on Christmas morning, one year ago today. It was one week into my admission into Beaufort Memorial Hospital with Covid-Pneumonia. I'm smiling because I hadn't shaved in over a week, and decided my Christmas gift to myself was to make myself look presentable.

I was kneeling at the sink with oxygen tube, trying to shave in their tepid water when my nurse came in. She started to fuss at me to get into bed but took pity on me and helped me shave my head. I was utterly out of strength to lift my arms at that point, and don't think I could have finished on my own. I don't remember her name, but I will never forget her kindness.

As I write this, a Sara Groves song comes to mind, titled simply, *Enough*, and now I am weepy:

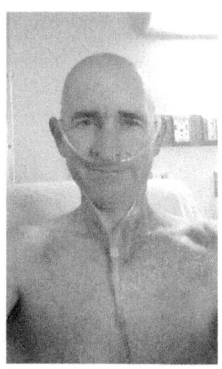

Really we don't need much
Just strength to believe
There's honey in the rock
There's more than we see
In these patches of joy
These stretches of sorrow
There's enough for today
There will be enough tomorrow.[23]

---

[23] Sara Groves, Julie Ann Lee, Sarah Dark, *Enough,* album Floodplain, 2015, track 5, Fair Trade Services, Brentwood, TN,
https://www.youtube.com/watch?v=DhW-HdXN0n8

Such a small thing, shaving my head. But it was enough. She took the extra time to show me love. To take care of me. It wasn't her job, and other patients were waiting. But I think maybe she thought I was going to die soon, alone in that room. So she made a snap decision to make my Christmas. And it made me feel like a new person.

So friends, maybe there is something small you can do for someone else today. It may seem insignificant to you, but it may be full of meaning for them. So please, take the time. Make the effort. Make someone's day. It's not hard, really.

Merry Christmas.

83. Questions for Joseph

At Christmas time, we talk and sing a lot about Mary, but do we ever give much thought to Joseph? God gave Joseph a mission, and it was a real doozy. It was to love and marry a woman who was already pregnant, and to be a daddy to her kid. That was it. To be husband and father, and to protect his little family from all dangers.

But I'll bet it was tough. This beautiful girl he is engaged to, whom he can't wait to marry – turns up pregnant with some ridiculous story. And while he is crying out to God, *"WHY ME?!?!?"*, God actually *ANSWERS* his prayer by sending an angel to tell him to not be afraid to marry her. And so he does. My guess is he did it the very next day. But people talk. Isn't that the *#1 Rule in religious circles – DON'T GET YOUR GIRLFRIEND PREGNANT?* Yet here she is, big belly, rushed wedding. Uh-huh. I'll bet there were broken friendships, relatives who wouldn't speak to them, and a whole lot of tears. I wonder, did *ANYONE* help the young couple, or were they on their own? I have so many questions! I wrote this song Christmas Day 2022, titled *Questions for Joseph.*

Joseph, did you know
How hard it was gonna be?
Did you love her, in spite of it all?
Did you cry so much you couldn't see?
Was her father mad?
Did he make a big scene?
Did you protest your innocence?
Did he find that hard to believe?

Sometimes God asks hard things.
He puts us there in the midst of the fire.
Somehow, obedience can be costly.
Through our tears, we cling to God.

Were the townspeople cruel?
Did you just walk away?
Did you tell them you heard from God?
Just what did they say?
Did she have a hard pregnancy?
Did you get your own place?
Did you wonder why God chose you
For this task, and filled you with his grace?

Sometimes God asks hard things.
He puts us there in the midst of the fire.
Somehow, obedience can be costly.
Through our tears, we cling to God.
Through our tears, we cling to God.

Go Joseph!
Love that woman – love her son,
This baby boy, the promised one —
Placed in your hands.
Go Joseph!
Be his Daddy – be her man.
Guard them and fulfill God's plan —
Your mission in life.

Sometimes God asks us hard things.
He puts us there in the midst of the fire.
Somehow, obedience can be costly.
Through our tears, we cling to God.

So maybe God has asked you a hard thing. (Or maybe you *MADE* things hard for yourself. It happens!) If this is you, I am here to tell you that God is *ABLE* to get you through this difficulty. 1 Corinthians 10:13 in *The Message* tells us:

> *No test or temptation that comes your way is*
> *beyond the course of what others have had to*
> *face. All you need to remember is that God will*
> *never let you down; he'll never let you be*
> *pushed past your limit; he'll always be there to*
> *help you come through it.*

So if this is you and you're struggling and need a friend – reach out. Sometimes God asks hard things. But he doesn't, as a general rule, ask you to go it alone. So reach out. Find someone.

Reach out.

84. New Year's Eve

Sometimes New Year's Eve can be a lonely night, filled with self-reflection, and perhaps feelings of loss. Of wondering where God is, or if He even cares? Yet the Bible references even babies in the womb as being part of God's plan, and on His mind. In Jeremiah 1:5 in *The Message,* God tells Jeremiah,

> *Before I shaped you in the womb,*
> *I knew all about you.*
> *Before you saw the light of day,*
> *I had holy plans for you:*
> *A prophet to the nations—*
> *that's what I had in mind for you.*

In fact, sometimes God even told the parents the child's name before the baby was even conceived!

- Abraham and Sarah (Genesis17:19)
- the prophet Isaiah and his wife (Isaiah 8:4)
- Zechariah and Elizabeth (Luke 1:13)
- Mary and Joseph (Luke 1:31), (Matthew 1:21)

Other times, God not only named children to be born in the far-off future, he also said what their role would be. The prophet Isaiah prophesied about the Messiah Immanuel (400 years in the future) in Isaiah 7:14, and about King Cyrus the Great, in Isaiah 44:28 *(NIV):*

> *Who says of Cyrus, "He is my Shepherd*
> *and will accomplish all that I please;*
> *he will say of Jerusalem, "Let it be rebuilt,"*
> *and of the temple, "Let its foundations*
> *be laid."*

Isaiah ministered between 740 and 686 BC. Cyrus was born in 600 BC, roughly 100 years later. And God said to him in Isaiah 45:4,

> *For the sake of Jacob my servant,*
>> *of Israel my chosen,*
> *I summon you by name and bestow on you a*
> *title of honor,*
>> *though you do not acknowledge me.*

Friends, I submit to you that *EVERY* child is known and loved by God, even babies in the womb. And that God has given us as parents, the *PRIVILEGE* of raising these little ones. These little ones God already has plans for. Embrace it!

And those who are not parents? You matter too! God knows your name, where you are, and what you are mixed up in.

> *Why would you ever complain, O Jacob,*
>> *or, whine, Israel, saying,*
> *"God has lost track of me.*
>> *He doesn't care what happens to me"?*
> *Don't you know anything?*
>> *Haven't you been listening?*
> *GOD doesn't come and go – God LASTS.*
>> *He's Creator of all you can see or*
> *imagine.*
> *He doesn't get tired out,*
>> *doesn't pause to catch his breath.*
> *And he knows EVERYTHING,*
>> *inside and out.*
> *He energizes those who get tired,*
>> *gives fresh strength to dropouts.*

For even young people tire and drop out,
young folk in their prime stumble and
fall.
But those who wait upon GOD get fresh
strength.
They spread their wings and soar like
eagles,
They run and don't get tired,
they walk and don't lag behind.
-Isaiah 40:27-31, The Message

New Year, new chance to start fresh with God. Happy New Year.

85. Just Come Home

When I was in first or second grade, I decided to run away from home. I packed my little backpack and was sitting at the end of the driveway with my Labrador Retriever Bonnie. I was mentally going through my checklist of stuff to bring, when I made the horrifying realization that I'm had forgotten to pack dog food. Moreover, that big dog could *EAT!* The whole backpack wasn't big enough to carry enough food for her. There was no way I could leave her behind, and I couldn't possibly bring her, so I decided to stay home. That big, beautiful dog probably saved my life that day.

There are many places in the Bible where God addresses prodigals. Jesus famously spoke in Luke 15 of the prodigal son who blew his father's inheritance on wine and women. The boy returned in fear and trembling, only to find his father waiting with outstretched arms.

But perhaps my favorite such passage is in Jeremiah 31:20-22 in *The Message*. It starts out like this:

> *"Oh! Ephraim is my dear, dear son, my child,*
> *in whom I take pleasure!*
> *Every time I mention his name, my heart bursts*
> *with longing for him!*
> *Everything in me cried out for him. Softly and*
> *tenderly I cry for him."*
>
> *GOD'S Decree.*

I love this imagery. It reminds me of Song of Solomon 5:4-6. Her lover thrusts his hand through the door, trying to release the lock. Heart pounding, she dresses and goes to the door to let him in, but despairs to find him gone.

I wrote *A Song for the Prodigal* based on these passages. It goes like this:

> *Oh my Love, I am longing*
> *For the day you return.*
> *My heart bursts*
> *When I hear your name.*
> *Come back home.*
> *Come back home.*
>
> *I hear your voice when I'm dreaming.*
> *Could it be that you're here?*
> *I check the door,*
> *But there's no one.*
> *Come back home.*
> *Come back home.*

Set up the signposts
To mark your way home.
Get a good map.
Lace up your boots.
Hit the road.
My arms are outstretched
With mercy and love!
Come as you are.
Come in your need.
Just come Home.

The way out is the way back.
Time to just pick up your feet
And shoulder your pack and now,
See the signs?
It's time to go.

Come as you are.
Come in your need.
Just come home.

Perhaps you're a prodigal. Estranged from family, or estranged from God, and you're considering coming home. Will you even be accepted? Is it worth the pain and effort? Has too much time passed? Can you handle one more rejection? It's New Year's Day. Perhaps I might suggest a New Year's Resolution for you?

Just come home.

86.   Leprosy and the Tent of Meeting

I've been thinking this morning about Naaman the Syrian, whose story is shared in 2 Kings 5. He was the top general for the king of Aram, and a Leper. His boss sent him to the king of Israel to be healed of his leprosy. The king of Israel (wisely) passed him off to Elisha. Leprosy ... was rather problematic. According to www.RisingStar.Outreach.org,

> *Once a person is infected with M. leprae the bacteria spreads through the body. It affects the skin, nerves, eyes, and other mucous membranes near the body's openings.*
>
> ***Because leprosy affects the nerves, if it is left untreated it can lead to serious loss of feeling or sensation. Injuries such as burns or cuts may go unnoticed because there are no pain signals to warn an individual of harm to his or her body.***
>
> *This loss of sensation in the extremities can lead to greater risk of severe infection and can lead to the shortening of toes and fingers which is due to re-absorption. Other serious signs of advanced and untreated leprosy may include paralysis and crippling of hands and feet, extreme light-sensitivity, blindness, loss of eyebrows, nose disfigurement, and skin ulcers.[24]*

---

[24] "Understanding the Disease." Rising Star Outreach: Lifting People with Leprosy. RisingStarOutreach.org/about-us/leprosy/

Elisha didn't bother to examine Naaman himself. Instead, he sent a servant to tell the great general to immerse himself in the dirty River Jordan, nearby. The general pitched a fit about the rivers back home being MUCH nicer and proceeded to stomp off. Eventually, his servants coaxed him into following the instructions of the holy man, and

> *His skin was healed; it was like the skin of a little baby. He was as good as new. He then went back to the Holy Man, he and his entourage, stood before him and said, "I now know beyond a shadow of a doubt that there is no God anywhere on earth other than the God of Israel. In gratitude, let me give you a gift."*
> *-2 Kings 5:14-15, The Message*

Elisha refuses the gift and sends him on his way home. But Elisha's servant Gehazi sneaked out and gave Naaman some contrived story about Elisha wanting something after all, so Naaman happily sent Gehazi back with two changes of nice clothes, and 150 lbs. of silver (!), and even sent a pair of his own servants back with Gehazi to carry the loot for him.

> *When they got to the fort on the hill, Gehazi took the gifts from the servants, stored them inside, then sent the servants back. He returned and stood before his master. Elisha said, "So, what have you been up to, Gehazi?"*
>
> *"Nothing much," he said.*
>
> *Elisha said, "Didn't you know I was with you in spirit when that man stepped down from his chariot to greet you? Tell me, is this a time to*

*look after yourself, lining your pockets with
gifts? Naaman's skin disease will now infect
you and your family with no relief in sight."*

*Gehazi walked away, his skin flaky and white
like snow.*

     -2 Kings 5:24-27, The Message

So here Gehazi did something slimy in secret, but God told
Elisha all about it. But God *DOES* this sometimes. I Corinthians
14: 24-25, quoted from *The New International Version*, tells us:

*But if an unbeliever or someone who does not
understand comes in while everybody is
prophesying, he will be convinced by all that he
is a sinner and will be judged by all, and the
secrets of his heart will be laid bare. So he will
fall down and worship God, exclaiming, "God
is really among you!"*

Years ago, I was part of a church where God was moving
powerfully for a season. We were having church six nights a
week and would often go to 11 pm. The worship leader would
come with two sets of songs, and then we would have to just
wing it. By the end of the service, 1/3 of the congregation was
being prayed for, 1/3 was praying, and 1/3 was passed out on
the floor. God's presence was *PALPABLE*. A sense of His
Holiness was overwhelming. So much so that I was having my
own private prayer time before going to church, fessing up to
any lingering sin in my life before even daring to get in the car
to go to church.

BECAUSE I WAS GOING TO CHURCH TO MEET WITH GOD.

And there was a very real possibility that the secrets of my heart would be revealed, as 1 Corinthians 14:24-25 pointed out. That's what happens when a prophetic people, a *LISTENING* people, start paying attention to **The - God - Who - Talks**. He shares stuff. Incidentally, the Tabernacle of the ancient Hebrews was called the Tent of Meeting. Not because it was the meeting house where the congregation met for services. Not at all. The Tent of Meeting was *where they would go to meet with God.*

That's what I want from going to church. Not great music, not an insightful sermon, not fellowship with other believers, although each of those things are important. I want to go to church to meet with God. That's what. Everything else is just gravy.

I also wonder about Naaman's leprosy. Why leprosy? Why not cancer, or Beri-Beri, or Alpha-Gal? Was it because leprosy destroys the sense of feeling, and so the body doesn't warn you that the fire is hot, and you are being burned? Elisha's servant was punished with leprosy after doing something shady and God told on him. Was God speaking to Gehazi the whole time, but he wanted to do it, so he ignored God and did it anyway? Did this spiritual lack of feeling, this lack of sensitivity to the voice of God become visually represented by a *PHYSICAL* lack of feeling, and the accompanying destruction? If I continue to ignore God's voice, will I develop spiritual leprosy- the lack of ability to feel and see and hear spiritually? I wonder.

As Sunday approaches, may we each get alone with God, and 'fess up. Clear the air. Clean the slate. And may we go to church to meet with God. And may He meet us there.

In the meeting place.

87. The Crisis

I'm thinking this morning about an encounter Jesus had with his disciples, recorded in John 21. By this time he had already been crucified and risen from the dead. He had already shown himself to them twice. He had already told Thomas to put his finger in the nail holes, and to put his hand in his side. He was real. It was all true.

Yet after all this, the disciples were *STILL* stressed enough that they went back to the life they lived BC- before Christ. Many of them had been fishermen. So when Peter declared that HE was going fishing, others came along. I mean, what *ELSE* could they do? So they fished all night and caught absolutely nothing. These professional fishermen were skunked. (It happens.)

Early in the morning, Jesus stood on the shore, but the disciples did not realize it was Jesus.

How often in our spiritual life is Jesus trying to do something, and we don't recognize it as him-- we don't recognize these circumstances or this "chance" encounter with someone as His doing? Pretty often would be my guess! So they shout to each other across the water:

> *"Catch anything?", shouts Jesus. "Nope!"*
> *"Throw your net on the other side of the boat!"*

Seriously? But they do so, and suddenly the net is filled with large fish, almost to breaking. They tow it to shore (no *WAY* all those beautiful fish would fit in the boat), and they find Jesus had already made a fire and *ALREADY* had bread and fish cooking on the fire for their breakfast.

He knew they were hungry, and provision had already been made. They didn't *NEED* to catch the 153 large fish, but Jesus was trying to make a point. He was proving, yet again, that he was able to meet their needs in impossible circumstances. (They had fished all night and caught nothing.) Now that he had their attention, he had stuff to tell them.

I think sometimes God *CREATES* crisis in our lives to see if we will turn to him. To see if He has our attention. Missiologist George Otis has a theory, and I think it's pretty good. He asks the question in his book *The Twilight Labyrinth: Why Does Spiritual Darkness Linger Where It Does?* (I'm paraphrasing), *"Why is the demonic activity so strong in high mountains and desert places? Is it because the devils enjoy a mountain view? No."*

He goes on to describe in place after place around the world, where a people group came to a crisis point. They had an insurmountable obstacle – a large mountain range or frightening desert to cross. Or perhaps they were confronted by a superior and intractable enemy. At this point of crisis, they had a choice. They could either turn to Creator God, who *STILL* loves them and cares about them, or they could make a pact with the demons. Those that turned to the demonic spirits for aid in their crisis took on themselves generations of bondage. And these are places of strong demonic power still today.

So friends, maybe *YOU* are in a Crisis. Maybe it's your own doing, from bad choices. But maybe, just *MAYBE*, God is orchestrating this crisis to get your attention and to put your focus on Him? (God has certainly done that in my life, and no, I am *NOT* going to tell you about it! At least not at this precise moment...) If this is you, stop fishing for a moment, sit down, and talk to God. See what he has to say.

And then see what He does.

88. The Lonely Road

What road are you on, and who is walking with you? There is a lot of spiritual imagery involving roads in the Bible. John the Baptist's commission was given 700 years before, in Isaiah 40:3 *(NIV)*, was that of road builder:

> *In the desert prepare the way for the Lord*
> *   make straight in the wilderness a*
> *highway for our God.*

or the passage in Jeremiah 31:21-22, quoted from *The Message:*

> *Set up signposts to mark your trip home.*
> *Get a good map.*
> *Study the road conditions.*
> *The road out is the road back.*
>
> *Come back, dear virgin Israel,*
> *come back to your hometowns.*
> *How long will you flit here and there,*
> *indecisive?*

*How long before you make up your fickle
mind?*

*God will create a new thing in this land:
a transformed woman will embrace the
transforming GOD!*

For me, roads represent a journey. Hardships. Struggle. The
movie *The Book of Eli*, starring Denzel Washington, is an
excellent example. But do you know that God walks these roads
with us? Zechariah 2:10 says, quoting from *The New
International Version*:

*"Shout and be glad, O daughter Zion. For I AM
COMING, and I WILL LIVE AMONG YOU,"
declares the LORD.*

Interestingly, Deuteronomy 23:12-14 in *The Message* instructs
the Hebrews that when they go outside the camp to relieve
themselves, that they should dig a hole and bury the excrement,
because "GOD, your God strolls through your camp;... Keep
your camp holy; don't permit anything indecent or offensive in
God's eyes." (Was he saying that He *PHYISICALLY* walked
through the encampment, and didn't want to step in it?) So what
does that mean for us today? Do we have indecent stuff in our
homes? On our TVs? (On our phones?) Ouch.

But I wonder, do we physically walk and talk with God
sometimes, and we don't even know it? The disciples sure did
on the road to Emmaus, recorded in Luke 24. It's a long walk
by American standards, seven miles, and they were walking and
talking with Jesus the whole way and didn't even recognize
him!

Genesis 3 tells us God physically walked in the Garden of Eden with Adam and Eve and talked with them in the cool of the day. We know God physically walked with them, because verse 8 notes that they heard the *sound* of God walking through the garden, and so they hid themselves. God also appeared to Abraham at the Trees of Mamre in Genesis 18, had dinner with him, and then walked down the road to Sodom. While we know that God is Omnipresent- He is everywhere, it seems to me that God is also *RIGHT HERE*. His very name is Immanuel -- "**God - With - Us**." Or put another way, "**God - Right - Here**."

But the passage about roads that really moves me is Psalm 84:5-7, quoted from *The Message:*

> *And how blessed all those in whom you live,*
> *whose lives become roads you travel;*
> *They wind through lonesome valleys, come*
> *upon brooks,*
> *discover cool springs and pools brimming with*
> *rain!*
> *God-traveled, these roads curve up the*
> *mountain,*
> *and at the last turn – Zion! God in full view!*

As I read this passage, a couple of scenes from *The Chronicles of Narnia* books come to mind, by C.S. Lewis. In *The Horse and His Boy*, the hero finds himself on a mountain path, in the dark and fog. He is lonely, and lost, and feeling rather sorry for himself. But a voice in the fog keeps pace with him and tells him the reality of his life – the whole back story. The voice tells him what was really going on behind the scenes in these moments of painful memory. The fog lifts, and he realizes it is the great lion Aslan, the Christ figure of the books. And he sees that he has been walking a cliff edge in the fog the entire night – the very cliff edge of doom! Yet Aslan has been walking this whole time between him and the edge of the cliff to keep him from falling. And the whole time Aslan is explaining that during each and every time of pain that the boy is recalling, Aslan himself was THERE, working behind the scenes for the boy's good. He just didn't know it.

In my own life, I keep a journal. I write down what is going on, and I pour my heart out to God. I sometimes draw pictures of things God shows me. One day I was stressing over painful things of the past that I didn't understand, and God showed me my journal, with the pages flipping in the wind from an open window. As the pages flipped, I saw paragraphs missing. Sometimes whole pages were missing from the story of my life. God was telling me that I was missing some information. I didn't know the whole story. He was working behind the scenes, and I wouldn't understand until the missing sections were filled in. And I believe someday He WILL fill me in. He will explain to me, like Aslan did to the boy in the fog, how He was working behind the scenes to protect me the whole time, even though I couldn't see it.

And how blessed all those in whom you live,
whose lives become roads you travel;

God was traveling that road with me, protecting me, and someday He'll fill in the missing pages – he will tell me all about it, and then I will understand. (And then I'll bawl my head off, odds are!)

They wind though lonesome valleys, come upon
brooks...

You know, the death of a loved one is a lonesome valley. And some of my friends have walked that valley recently. It totally sucks. This verse reminds me of a scene in another of *The Chronicles of Narnia* books, *The Silver Chair*. It is time for the two children to go home, and they find themselves in Aslan's country. They come upon a quiet brook, and there, under the water, is the body of their old friend, King Caspian. He is dead, and his long grey beard is moving gently in the current.

As they are grieving, Aslan appears and tells them to select a large thorn and to prick his paw. As he holds it over the body of the dead king, a great drop of blood falls into the water. As the children watch, aging is reversed and the dead king is transformed before their eyes into the young king they remember from their adventures together, and he steps alive from the stream!

Maybe you are in that lonesome valley right now, grieving. But this valley road is God-traveled, and this grief is not the end.

> *God-traveled, these roads curve up the mountain,*
> *And at the last turn – Zion! God in full view!*

We don't see the whole picture. As we turn corners in our lives, we continue to see new peaks in the distance, and the road continues on. But someday, we will round what *REALLY IS* the final bend in the road and we will be met with an overwhelming sight. Zion! God in full view!

People talk about going to heaven as "going to our eternal reward." and that's true enough. But that's not really the reward part. The reward part is that *GOD IS THERE*. That's the reward. ***"God in full view!"***

If you are grieving right now, and want someone to talk to, you have my ear. Reach out.

May God travel your road today.

89. Have Mercy!

In Moscow in 1941, the day came when the twenty thousand German army prisoners were to be marched through the streets in front of a population who had borne the burden of their cruelty. The pavements were crowded that day, mainly with women and children, those who had borne the brunt of the terrible suffering. Most of their men folk were dead. Almost everyone had lost a husband, a son; and many had lost mothers, sisters, daughters because of this army, these people who were going to march down this street. You can imagine something of the atmosphere that day. At last they were going to see their hated enemy. There were angry mutterings and shouts of hate as the first of that defeated army, the Generals, prisoners yet still arrogant, strutted at the fore. People spat in the snow.

But then came the soldiers. And they were just boys really. Shuffling through the snow, their feet frostbitten, wrapped in newspapers. Many of them were on makeshift crutches, others being led blind by their mates. As silence fell, and all you could hear was the shuffling of feet and the thumping of crutches. The shuffling of a defeated army of broken young boys.

Then there was a sudden movement. A woman, an old babushka, pushed herself through the crowd to the Russian soldiers guarding the pavement and said, "Let me through." Then this bent old woman rushed across to one of the gaunt German prisoners, and everybody held their breath. What was she going to do? Slap him? Spit on him?

*She reached into her shawl and took out a crust of black bread, which she then pushed awkwardly into the pocket of the soldier, so exhausted that he was tottering on his feet. And all of a sudden from every direction, women began to hand over perhaps a cigarette, perhaps some bread, perhaps a piece of fish; and somehow the hatred was gone, enemies had ceased to be enemies. Why? Because one person, such an ordinary person, intervened into that cycle of hate and revenge with a simple act of pardoning love. That's all."[25]
Sometimes, what's really needed is kindness.*

[25] Yevgeny Yevtushenko, A Precocious Autobiography, trans. Andrew R. MacAndrew (New York: Dutton, 1963)
https://www.amazon.com/Precocious-Autobiography-Yevgeny-Yevtushenko/dp/B000K09LJG

90.   The Black Horse

Something has been on my heart lately, and I wanted to share it with you. I keep opening scripture to passages on famine. Here are a couple of examples, from Acts 7:11-12 and Acts 11:28-30. In this first passage, in Acts Chapter 7, the martyr Stephen is recounting to the Jewish leaders their religious heritage – the story of God's deliverance so long ago:

> *Later a famine descended on that entire region,*
> *stretching from Egypt to Canaan, bringing*
> *terrific hardship. Our hungry fathers looked*
> *high and low for food, but the cupboard was*
> *bare. Jacob heard there was food in Egypt...*
> *   -Acts 7:11-12, The Message*

This second passage in Acts Chapter 11, describes how once again, centuries later, God warned his people of approaching famine. They heard the Word, they made preparation, and then they acted.

> *It was about this same time that some prophets*
> *came to Antioch from Jerusalem. One of them*
> *named Agabus stood up one day and, prompted*
> *by the Spirit, warned that a severe famine was*
> *about to devastate the country. (The famine*
> *eventually came during the rule of Claudius.)*
> *So the disciples decided that each of them*
> *would send whatever they could to their fellow*
> *Christians in Judea to help out. They sent*
> *Barnabas and Saul to deliver the collection to*
> *the leaders in Jerusalem...*
> *   -Acts 11:27-30, The Message*

As I read this passage, God showed me the scene from Ruth Chapter 1- Naomi and Ruth hurrying, scarves on their heads, scurrying to Bethlehem because they heard that God had visited His people with *FOOD*. There was once again bread in Bethlehem – the House of Bread. And, *NOT* coincidentally, Jesus the Messiah, who called himself **The - Bread - Of - Life**, was born in *BETHLEHEM … The - House - of - Bread.* (Write that down.)

Friends, God talks. And sometimes He provides warnings of trouble to come. Amos 3:7 in *The Message* tells us:

> *The fact is GOD, the Master, does nothing*
> *without first telling his prophets the whole story.*

I believe that this *IS* one of those times. long ago, God gave pagan king Pharaoh a dream of impending famine so he would prepare, and in so preparing, save Joseph's family. And I am hearing the same thing from various people today, in unrelated ministries, that God is telling them hard times and famine are coming. And I believe it to be true.

In the natural, the sequence is war, famine, and pestilence-- usually in that order. War disrupts food supply, both in the growing and in the distribution. This leads to famine. War also disrupts sanitation by moving people away from their support systems and then malnutrition makes them extra susceptible to disease. And so disease begins to spread, much more quickly than would have been the case without the preceding factors. It is estimated that 40% of the world wheat supply comes from Russia and Ukraine, and these supplies are already disrupted. Drought has affected other crops and prices worldwide are surging. We still have plenty of food on the shelves here in 'Merica, but I firmly believe it is a short-term bounty.

So how then should we live? I believe that the Christian response is to prepare for hard times by heeding God's warnings by stocking up. But more importantly, *to cultivate a spirit of generosity*. Not to build a higher wall, or a deeper bunker. But rather *to set a bigger table*. To be prepared to bring strangers to our own tables. And I'm not talking about feeding the homeless. (That problem is ongoing.) I'm talking about our friends and neighbors.

In the preceding chapter, I shared a true story from World War II of a crowd in Moscow watching a scarecrow column of German prisoners of war, marching into captivity. One old Russian grandmother rushed up and stuffed a crust of stale bread in a starving soldier boy's pocket. She started a movement of women towards the boys, hearts moved with compassion, who each did what they could.

I believe days like this are coming again to America, with hardships not seen since our Civil War. So friends, please pray about this for yourselves. Ask God for yourselves if this is true. If this is coming. And if so, what would He have YOU to do.

So pray, buy a little extra when you go to the store, and go make friends with your neighbors. I think we're all going to need each other this year.

91. No Peeking!

A few days ago, I noticed that God had stopped talking to me about a long-term concern, and I was asking Him "Why was that?" In response, God showed me two workmen, stagehands, carrying a curtain across the stage, blocking my view. When I asked God what the vision meant, 2 Kings 4:27 in the *NIV* came to mind. In this passage, a woman in anguish has come to the prophet Elisha:

> *When she reached the man of God at the*
> *mountain, she took hold of his feet. Gehazi*
> *came over to push her away, but the man of*
> *God said, "Leave her alone! She is in bitter*
> *distress, but the LORD has hidden it from me*
> *and has not told me why."*

God was telling me that, for His purposes, I was not allowed to watch while the stage was being set for the next act. My job was to sit my butt in the chair and WAIT. I also noticed that the curtain wasn't lowered from the ceiling, indicating the play was over. Not at all. This is just a scene change, so I was not to get excited.

I am reminded of the story of the man walking by the lunatic asylum and hearing the patients behind the wooden fence chanting *"Twenty-one! Twenty-one! Twenty-one! Twenty-one!"* His curiosity aroused, he put his face to a knothole in the fence to see what was going on and was immediately poked in the eye by one of the patients... *"Twenty-TWO!"* the inmates gleefully shouted. *"Twenty-TWO! Twenty-TWO! Twenty-TWO!"*

So if this is you, and God has closed something off to your vision or understanding, kindly resist the urge to peek around the curtain. Allow Him to set the stage without interference.

TWENTY-TWO!!!

92. The Timing of Promises

This morning I was turning some things over in my mind that God has been showing me – things I didn't understand (and still don't.) I was asking God about timing, and he showed me a scene from *The Voyage of the Dawn Treader* (the C.S. Lewis book, not the terrible movie.) He showed me Aslan and Lucy having an intimate conversation, off in the distance.

> *"Please Aslan," asked Lucy,*
> *"What do you call soon?"*
> *"I call all times soon..."*[26]

They were alone in the distance, too far away for me to eavesdrop on, but I knew what was being said because I am familiar with the book. I think the fact that Aslan and Lucy were distant from me is part of the interpretation of the vision. They were alone with each other. This place of intimacy – this *"Alone-ness"* – is where He is known to talk to us. Awhile back, I was stressing over time passing, and God spoke to my heart,

> *"Do hours and years mean anything to me? Is ANYTHING too hard for me?"*

---

[26] C. S. Lewis, *The Voyage of the Dawn Treader* (London: Geoffrey Bles, 1952)

God was quoting Jeremiah 32:27 to me. In context, right in the middle of the Babylonian siege, God tells the prophet Jeremiah that his cousin was coming to ask him to buy his piece of land, and that he was to do so. Moreover, he was to pay in silver, have the deed notarized, and put copies in long-term storage. This made no sense! So Jeremiah protested to God about the pointlessness of these instructions:

> *"See how the siege ramps are built to take the city. Because of the sword, famine, and plague, the city will be handed over to the Babylonians who are attacking it. What you said has happened, as you now see. And though the city will be handed over to the Babylonians, you, O Sovereign LORD say to me, 'Buy the field with silver and have the transaction witnessed.'"*
>
> *Then the word of the LORD came to Jeremiah: "I am the LORD, the God of all mankind. Is anything too hard for me?"*
> *-Jeremiah 32:24-27, (NIV)*

God was telling Jeremiah that what he could see with his eyes ... was irrelevant. God was in charge. And God was going to accomplish his own purposes, regardless of the current reality.

Lana Vawser wrote in her December 28, 2022 post *"Time is Being Redeemed"* on www.LanaVawser.com:

> *"... This year I had one of the most profound encounters of my life where I heard the Lord thunder 'BEGIN AGAIN.' I knew he was speaking over seasons and speaking to Time. In that moment, the realization that time is but a*

resource to Him and Time bows to Him
surrounded me strongly..."

So perhaps God has made promises to you in your own life. But years (or decades?) have passed, and you have despaired of ever seeing fulfillment. And the serpent from the Garden of Eden is whispering in your ear as he did to Eve, "Has God *REALLY* said...?" But perhaps God would say to you in response,

"Do hours and years mean anything to me? Is
ANYTHING too hard for me?"

93. Jesus Revolution

Last night I watched a good movie, *Jesus Revolution*.[27] I find it interesting that while Rotten Tomatoes gave it a 60% score, the viewer rating (the popcorn score) is 99%!!! Hahahahah! (This alone is a great reason to watch it.)

I didn't enjoy it because of the memories it called up. There is a scene where the hippies showed up in church and some of the church members left. I think that had I been there, my church people in the churches I grew up in may have been the ones walking out. And I probably would have joined them. I still have an aversion to those who are ... different. If I am being totally honest, I barely understand myself. And those recognizably different? Deep inside, they frighten me.

---

[27] Jesus Revolution, directed by Jon Erwin and Brent McCorkle (Lionsgate, 2023), https://jesusrevolution.movie

I also saw examples of really bad parenting, and I recalled some bad parents I have known, and my heart aches for their damaged kids – damage that followed them into adulthood. I think about the job I am doing as a parent of teenagers, and I wonder – am I doing it right? Am I hurting, or am I helping?

I assume the movie is historically accurate, since one of the main characters is still alive and involved, but what I think they really get right is *PEOPLE*. Real people. One of the main characters, the Jesus figure, rubbed me wrong – not because of his acting, but because he reminded me so very much of someone I was once close to. Someone who came out of terrible background, became a Christian, was used mightily in ministry ... and then went back to his old lifestyle. Someone who is long gone from my life, and from this earth. He is past my ability to find out what went wrong. He had so much *INFLUENCE* on my life, and now he is gone, and I question what of him was real, what was God, and what was flesh. And I start to ask myself, *"Am I Real?"*

Public baptisms feature prominently in the movie, and I think of the children and teenagers baptized in our churches, who are adults now. Except many are not in church and they no longer think of themselves as Christians. What went wrong? How did they lose their faith? Was it never real to start with? These hippies were looking for *REALITY*, and they found it in Jesus.

I was raised in church. We were there Sunday morning, Sunday night, Wednesday night – every time the doors were open. I went to a Christian school, K-12. I memorized scripture, and prayed a prayer at vacation bible school when I was 7, and "asked Jesus into my heart." I remember the grass was green and the sky was blue and the birds were singing and it felt

AMAZING. But then I became religious. By the time I got to high school, I measured my Christianity by what I *DIDN'T* do. And it was a pretty long list. I knew a lot *ABOUT* God, but I didn't know him personally. There was not real relationship. It's kinda like my relationship with George Washington. I *BELIEVE* in George Washington. He existed. He did great things and is much revered. There is zero doubt in my mind that he led us to victory in the Great Patriotic War (sorry, Russian joke) and was our first president. But I don't know him. We never talk ...

But then I went off to college, far from home, and there were no more rules. Nobody cared. Life was hard as a first semester military cadet, and I had no real relationship with God to fall back on. I was utterly miserable. But the pastor of my Parents' church challenged us to read through the Bible in a year, and so I started reading. Simply as an intellectual exercise. "You say you believe the Bible, but have you actually read it?" he challenged us. And so I started reading. And God started to change my life. And then God started bringing people to me who were *Real*. Who trusted God, not just for eternal security, but in their everyday life. The scene in the movie where the group prayed that God would fix the car reminds me of my friend who prayed for good parking spaces – and got them. Or the friend who prayed over another friend who had been told she had miscarried – and then the baby was born healthy.

I learned that God *TALKS*, and that he heals. God became *REAL* to me for the first time at college, after I had spent my whole life in church. So is that our problem, that we learn *ABOUT* God in church, but He isn't real to us there? How do we change that?

I was thinking this morning about the movie and about the free love atmosphere in the movie, and about everyone sitting around stoned and loving everyone, and I was disgusted. And then God brought Jeremiah 31: 2-3 to mind, quoted from *The Message:*

> *This is the way GOD put it:*
>
> *"They found grace out in the desert,*
> *these people who survived the killing.*
> *Israel, out looking for a place to rest,*
> *met God out looking for them!"*
>
> *God told them,*
>
> *"I've never quit loving you, and I never will.*
> *Expect Love, Love, and more Love!"*

Yeah, this movie made me uncomfortable.

You should definitely watch it.

94.   The Trials of Bathsheba

I have been ruminating lately on Bathsheba and her family relationships after her second marriage. 2 Samuel 11:26-27 in *The New International Version* tells us:

> *When Uriah's wife heard that her husband was dead, she mourned for him. After the time of her mourning was over, David had her brought to his house and she became his wife and bore him a son. But the thing David had done displeased the LORD...*

We usually focus on David in this story, and that's a big lesson to be sure, but do we care about Bathsheba and her hardships? Modern Judaism observes Shivah, a 7-day period of mourning and Shloshim, a 30-day period of mourning. It is not recorded which one this was. However, I would venture that her heart was still in mourning for her lost husband when she was brought to David's home and quietly married to him. I personally don't let go of people easily. (It took me five years to get over the first woman I ever loved, but eventually I set her up with my best friend and they have been married for 24 years. God bless her and keep her...)

But what I am really wondering is, how did the other women treat Bathsheba? David was already married to at least three other women, and presumably had concubines as well. Six sons were already born to him in Hebron from six different women (2 Samuel 3:2-5). So here is the new girl, and she's pregnant with their husband's baby. And now *SHE's* married to him too. Oh goody.

So how did they react? Did they welcome her with love and compassion as a sister-wife? Or did they slut-shame her, leaving her alone to cope by herself with her grief and new pregnancy?

Some time ago, I was talking hypotheticals with a friend about marriage and pregnancy. I commented that I would have married my wife even if she had been carrying another man's baby. (She wasn't.) His response is that if he were in that situation, he would want her to have the baby first before he married her. *"Really??? Do you love her or not?"* Love is shown not just in words and feelings, but in care for someone. I am thinking of Joseph, who took tender care of pregnant Mary, even though the baby wasn't his. There is *NO WAY* that I would want a woman I loved to go through pregnancy and childbirth and parenting a newborn alone. I couldn't do it.

Love is shown in serving someone. Do you know any single moms? Love on them. Serve them. Help with the kids. Do their laundry. Clean their kitchen. Learn their story. Bring them to church with you. And the same goes for married moms with little kids, and for military wives whose husbands are deployed. And really, to *ALL* parents of little kids. Be helpful. Be Jesus to them.

Maybe you're involved in sexual sin and are at the spiritual *"Now what?"* stage. Does God still love me? Is my life over? Can God ever use me again? I really love what Micah 7:18 in *The Message* has to say:

> *Who is the god who can compare with you —*
> *wiping the slate clean of guilt,*
> *Turning a blind eye, a deaf ear,*
> *to the past sins of your purged and precious*
> *people?*
> *You don't nurse your anger*
> *and don't stay angry long.*
> *For mercy is your specialty.*
> *That's what you love most.*

Maybe you're living together but not married. There is an easy spiritual solution for that. How about making it official? My church in Beaufort South Carolina is doing a bunch of weddings on the last Sunday in February, for people just like you. People who love each other but haven't gotten around to the ceremony. Many girls (all girls?) dream since childhood about having the "perfect" wedding. Some save items on Pinterest and plan their dream wedding in their head *ad nauseum*, often without even being in a relationship! But really, the important part isn't the perfection of the wedding, it's the being together, committed as husband and wife. There is no need to spend a bundle on a fancy wedding.

As for David and Bathsheba, their first child died. That was absolutely brutal for them both. I have never lost a child, and I can't imagine that kind of pain. But there is a really beautiful postscript to their story:

> *Then David went and comforted his wife*
> *Bathsheba. And when he slept with her, they*
> *conceived a son. When he was born they named*
> *him Solomon. God had a special love for him*
> *and sent word through Nathan the prophet to*
> *name him Jedidiah, "Beloved of the Lord."*
> *-2 Samuel 12:24-25, The Message*

David and Bathsheba went on to have other sons and daughters, and that boy, that "consolation pregnancy," grew up to become King Solomon. Go God!

So if you're stuck in sexual sin, your life isn't over. Fix it and walk on. God has big plans for you, so don't quit now. If you're a single mom, and barely keeping it together, reach out to someone!

See what the faithful God will do!

95. Out of Control

I have stuff going on in my personal life, and I am in a place of significant uncertainty. (More news later.) Psalm 42:5-8 is resonating:

Why are you downcast, O my soul? Why so
disturbed within me?
Put your hope in God, for I will yet praise him,
my Savior, and my God.

My soul is downcast within me:
therefore I will remember you...

Deep calls to deep in the roar of your
waterfalls.
All your waves and breakers have swept over
me.

By day the LORD directs his love, at night his
song is with me—
a prayer to the God of my life.

I quoted this from *The New International Version*, the *NIV*, but I also like how other translations convey these thoughts. Different translations are frequently similar, but sometimes they convey a different nuance. *The Message* puts it:

When my soul is in the dumps, I rehearse
everything I know of you...

Not just remembering, but *REHEARSING*; telling yourself over and over, so you don't forget. I am thinking of Aslan's instructions to Jill in *The Chronicles of Narnia* book, *The Silver Chair*, by C.S. Lewis:

> *Remember, remember, remember the Signs.*
> *Say them to yourself when you wake in the*
> *morning and when you lay down at night. And*
> *whatever strange things may happen to you, let*
> *nothing turn your mind from following the*
> *Signs...*[28]

Then there is the "deep calls to deep" line. It's beautiful, to be sure. But what does it MEAN, exactly? *The New Living Translation* gives us a clue:

> *I hear the tumult of the raging seas as your*
> *waves and surging tide sweep over me.*

Some of you have lost spouses recently (or have lost loves, and today is Valentine's Day.) The waves of Grief are *deafening* for you right now. Or perhaps you feel overwhelmed and tumbling in the breakers in other ways. Your life is out of control, or perhaps *BEYOND* your control.

Last night I had a couple of dreams. In the first, I was on stage at church, playing with the worship team, except not all the strings were on my guitar yet and the electronics weren't hooked up right, but *THE SONG WAS STARTING AND I WASN'T READY!* In the second dream, I had been tasked with finishing a ride patterned after the ejection seat of a fighter jet. You put your head back against the headrest, pull the rings between your legs, and then you rocket upward. I was under the seat, trying

---

[28] C. S. Lewis, *The Silver Chair (London: Geoffrey Bless, 1953)*

to finish the wiring and the safetys, but the guest was ready to strap in, I was supposed to test it on myself first, warning lights were flashing, and the countdown to launch was blaring, *AND I WASN'T READY!*

The dreams were a matched set with the same meaning. Things are *In-Motion*, and I am not ready. But for some things, like the loss of a loved one, there *IS* no ready ... You just have to pick up the guitar and play ...

I am reminded of a couple of visions God gave me awhile back, where I was driving a car down a narrow road with obstacles in the way that I had to dodge. Suddenly, my speed picked up because *GOD* was mashing the gas pedal. We were going uncomfortably fast, but God was telling me that *HE* controlled the timetable and would accelerate things at his pace, not mine. Later, God showed me the same scene again, only this time I was in a top-fuel dragster. God had His foot on the gas pedal, and we were *ROCKETING* down the road.

Things were In-Motion, I was *NOT* in control, and I didn't like it one bit, no sir! But sometimes God puts us in these situations. Where we are not ready. Where we are not in control. I was stressing to God last week about the future, emotionally hyperventilating about things. *"But God, what about THIS??? AND what about THAT???"* In response, God spoke to my heart and said simply, *"You're just going to have to trust Me."*

> *When my soul is in the dumps, I rehearse*
> *everything I know of you.*

Remember the signs.

96.   More Than Enough

There is a (Chinese?) curse that says, "May you live in interesting times." My inner response is, *"NO, NO, NO! Boring is good! Boring is NICE!..."* Well, my times are getting a little more interesting.

A few weeks ago, I noticed a strange lump on my left armpit. It was growing, and then a lump developed in my right armpit. We had an ultrasound and a blood test, and the doctors noted inflamed lymph nodes in my groin and neck as well, and an elevated white blood cell count, indicating my body is fighting something. I have also started having night sweats and severe acid reflux. All of these put together suggest Lymphoma, so yesterday I had a biopsy from the lump in my left armpit. Lab results will take 3-5 days, but the doctor said it was probably lymphoma. Encouragingly, he said that "if you HAVE to have something, this is the one to have, because it is very treatable."

The procedure itself wasn't bad. No worse than a bad day at the dentist. But I got a serious migraine headache on the way home and became instantly nauseated with the first bite of chicken for lunch. (You ladies out there – is this what the first trimester of pregnancy is like?) I had a good cry, went to bed, and then projectile vomited all over the bathroom. I got the wall, the floor, the toilet seat ... Absolutely lovely. But then I felt better and took a nap. I am on light duty today while my armpit heals, and then it is back to work.

But where is God in all this, you ask?

Before I went into the hospital with Covid, God warned me a big trial was coming, and when. I was grateful. I believe this is another one of those times, when He is warning me to get me ready.

Earlier this week, he showed me a couple of things while I was thinking and praying about my situation. First, I saw an AA battery, lying on its side, with its top missing and what looked like scorch marks on the inside. It reminded me of a tank that had been hit by a missile and blown its turret as all the ammunition inside cooked off. I interpreted that vision to mean that I will feel "burnt out."

Then, God showed me a huge mason jar of "Survival Soup." Many Preppers often make up soup in advance, with all the dry ingredients pre-mixed. All you do is add water. As I watched, a big spoon dipped into the mason jar, and then dished the contents into a cast iron skillet where food was cooking. The skillet was full of food, and it looked GOOD. But I also noticed that even though the skillet was full of food cooking, the mason jar was hardly depleted.

What I think God was telling me was that He was going to provide for me. There would be *More Than Enough*. Yes, I was going to feel burned out. But he had *AMPLE* stores and would supply what I needed. He is more than enough. And I don't need to worry.

Game plan: I am resting today and will go back to work tomorrow. I plan to continue going to the gym regularly. My arm is a little sore, but I feel good otherwise. I need to make hay while the sun shines, as the farmers say. Prayer is appreciated! For wisdom, for strength, for courage, for HEALING, and for my family. I will keep you posted.

But God is More Than Enough, and I am at peace.

193

97. Pain

I encountered this quote again after reading it many years ago, and it rattled me:

> *David was caught in a very uncomfortable position; however, he seemed to grasp a deep understanding of the unfolding drama in which he had been caught. He seemed to understand something that few of even the wisest men of his day understood. Something that in our day, even when men are wiser still, even fewer understand.*
>
> *And what was that?*
>
> *God did not have -- but wanted very much to have -- men and women who would live in pain.*
>
> *God wanted a broken vessel."* [29]
> *-- Gene Edwards, A Tale of Three Kings.*

Oh my goodness! Some people are *INTO* pain. I am *NOT* one of those people. I am thinking of the scene in Job 1 and 2 of the heavenly court, where God says to Satan, "Have you considered my servant Job?" I wonder, if Job could have been present at that moment, would he have been jumping up and down in the back, waving his hands, trying to get God's attention?

---

[29] Gene Edwards, *A Tale of Three Kings: A Study in Brokenness* (Carol Stream, IL: Tyndale House, 1992).

"No No No No NOOOOOOOooooooooooo!
PLEASE pick someone else?!?!"

I surely would have. But notice his actual response? His children were all dead, his wealth was gone, he had nothing left, but we are told that his first response was the traditional one: to tear his robe and shave his head.

But then he added a step. He fell to the ground in *WORSHIP*. Job 1:21 *(NIV)* records his response to this greatest of calamities:

> *"Naked I came from my mother's womb, and naked I'll depart. The LORD gave, and the LORD has taken away; may the name of the LORD be praised."*

Sometimes pain is part of this life's journey, and sometimes shame too. This past week was a little rough. I had the biopsy on Wednesday and became violently sick from the anesthesia. Then on Thursday, I had to have hemorrhoid surgery. Oh the indignity!!! But as I was walking into the doctor's office and contemplating the embarrassment to come, God reminded me of Philippians 2: 6-8, quoted from *The New Living Translation:*

> *Though he was God, he did not think equality with God as something to cling to. Instead, he gave up his divine privileges; he took the humble position of a slave and was born as a human being. When he appeared in human form, he humbled himself in obedience to God and died a criminal's death on the cross.*

Gene Edwards commented in one of his books on this stunning turn of events by imagining the scene in heaven when the angels learn of God HUMBLING himself to be born a man – of the angels agape in horror at the thought. *"A man in the form of a ROACH would be more seemly!"* But God did this for me. And hung naked on the cross. Who am I to fret over one of life's little indignities?

As I think about it, some Christian leaders are all about the honors. The number of members. The money. The glory. The television audience. But often, for true Christian leaders, it's the opposite. Paul writes in I Corinthians 4:9, quoted from *The New International Version*:

> *For it seems to me that God has put us apostles*
> *on display at the end of the procession, like*
> *men condemned to die in the arena. We have*
> *been made a spectacle to the whole universe, to*
> *angels, as well as to men.*

That imagery of bedraggled prisoners hauled along at the tail end of the line, marching to their execution in the Colosseum – suggests that pain and discomfort just might come with the package. We usually think of pain as a sign of God's displeasure. His punishment. But what if actually, it's a sign of his Grace on us – **like maybe He trusts us with it?** That there is more going on than just our pain?

I am thinking of pastor Richard Wurmbrand, who wrote of his imprisonment by the communists in Romania. He described the informal deal he and some of the other Christian prisoners had with the guards in his book *Tortured for Christ*:

It was strictly forbidden to preach to other prisoners. It was understood that whoever was caught doing this received a severe beating. A number of us decided to pay the price for the privilege of preaching, so we accepted their [the communists] terms. It was a deal; we preached, and they beat us. We were happy preaching. They were happy beating us, so everyone was happy.[30]

And we are afraid to talk about Jesus because of what someone might SAY to us?

98. Cancer

Today has been interesting. I use a Cloud service called OneDrive. Today it showed me a bracelet that quoted Psalm 46:10 –

"Be still and know that I am God."

God used that bracelet years ago with me when I was begging Him to do something in a certain area. He didn't answer. Finally, in frustration, I opened Instagram to a post by www.mintandlily.com and I was staring at this cuff bracelet. God was telling me to stop Striving, and to trust Him.

---

[30] Richard Wurmbrand, *Tortured for Christ, 50th Anniversary Edition* (Colorado Springs CO, David C. Cook, 2017).

And here we are again. So I opened One Drive, noted the image (Okay, God), then opened my Bible at random to Luke 2:22-23, in *The Message:*

> *[Jesus] went on, 'It is necessary that the Son of Man proceed to an ordeal of suffering, be tried and found guilty by the religious leaders, high priests, and religion scholars, be killed, and on the third day be raised up alive.*
>
> *Then he told them what they could expect for themselves: "Anyone who intends to come after me has to let me lead. You're not in the driver's seat -- I am. Don't run from suffering, embrace it. Follow me and I'll show you how."*

Okay, embrace suffering, don't run from it, right, right. Not my favorite scripture passage, but probably just random, right? Next I opened again at random and was staring at Job 13: 20-21, where Job is entreating God in the middle of his agony:

> *"Please, God, I have two requests: grant them, so I know I count with you:*
> *First, lay off the afflictions, the terror is too much for me..."*

Okay, God. This is about my pending cancer diagnosis, right? Give me courage! Then God spoke to my heart these words:

> *"My grace is sufficient."*

God was quoting 2 Corinthians 12:8-9a *(NIV)* to me. In context, the Apostle Paul, the same Paul who performed incredible healing miracles, had a physical affliction himself. Paul writes:

*Three times I pleaded with the Lord to take it
away from me. But he said to me, "My grace is
sufficient for you, for my power is made perfect
in weakness."*

Okay, God. My heart was at peace. A couple of hours later, I finally got the expected phone call. The doctor said I have Non-Hodgkin's Lymphoma, and that an oncologist would be calling me to set up an appointment. So it's *ON*. God had been preparing me for it for the past few weeks, and again this morning, so the call itself wasn't devastating.

Even so, I still had a breakdown this afternoon. In a moment, I felt emotionally drained. Like it was the end of everything. It came on so fast – in a matter of seconds. And in my despair, God quickly spoke to my heart John 16:33,

*"Be of good courage, I have overcome the
world."*

Jesus was with his disciples on the night of his betrayal. He had a lot to say to them, but then he told them *WHY* he was telling them all these things.

*"I have told you these things, so that in me you
may have peace. In this world you will have
trouble but take heart! I have overcome the
world." (NIV)*

So God was telling me that this is going to hurt. But that He is there with me. As our soldiers and marines say, it's time to embrace the suck. But, God is here, and He is asking me to *TRUST* Him.

Be still and know that I am God. (And embrace the suck.)

99.   The Good and the Bad

Anyone else here (constantly?) thinking about food? No? Well yesterday morning, God showed me food. A half-eaten chimichanga, specifically. Goop (sauce?) was oozing out, and there were unidentifiable chunks on the plate. As I watched, I saw myself taking the fork to carefully eat every last bite.

"God, what does this mean?" My thoughts wandered to my time in the hospital with Covid when I was ravenous from the steroids. I felt like the Marvel Movie character Venom, prowling around muttering to himself, *"FOOD!"* When my dinner tray came, I ate every bite, even hated vegetables such as cauliflower. I was hungry, *AND* I wanted to get well. So I ate it all. At first, I thought this was about nutrition. (I had to give up red meat 3 years ago because I got a stupid allergy called Alpha-gal syndrome from a tick bite. Now I am allergic to the meat of all mammals.) Giving up beef and bacon was tough, but now I have to cut back on sugar too? This sucks!

But as I think about the vision, a second interpretation comes to mind – taking the bad in with the good. I recalled Job's response to his hardship – *"Shall we accept good from God, and not trouble?"* Okay, that made sense. But then I looked up that passage in Job 2:7-10 in *The Message* and did a double take. The context was physical suffering:

> *Satan left God and struck Job with terrible*
> *sores. Job had ulcers and scabs from head to*
> *foot. They itched and oozed so badly that he*
> *took a piece of broken pottery to scrape*

*himself, then went and sat on a trash heap,
among the ashes.*

*His wife said, "Still holding on to your precious
integrity are you? Curse God and be done with
it!"*

*He told her, "You're talking like an empty-
headed fool. We take the good days from God –
why not also the bad days?"*

*Not once through all of this did Job sin. He
said nothing against God.*

Some of you are asking how I'm feeling. Honestly, I feel GREAT! I have swollen lymph nodes in my armpits, my groin, and my neck, but they don't hurt. At the most, they are mildly uncomfortable with pressure. The doctor referred me to an oncologist for treatment, but that hasn't happened yet. They tell me I have Nodal Marginal Zone B-cell lymphoma. According to www.cancercenter.com:

*This is another rare type of cancer, accounting
for about 1 percent of all lymphomas,
according to ASCO. It tends to begin in the
lymph nodes and remains there, though it
sometimes spreads to the bone marrow.
Treatment options are similar to those used to
treat follicular lymphoma: radiation alone for
early-stage disease, or chemotherapy, targeted
therapy and/or radiation therapy as the cancer
progresses.*

I don't know which treatments I will receive, but I expect it to be chemotherapy, plus some other things. (The potential treatment I fear most is a bone marrow transplant.) I am not afraid of dying, but pain is not high on my priority list! Please pray for me that I will be able to get lots of work done before the cancer symptoms or the treatment makes physical work difficult. I feel great right now, but pain is coming, and that's okay. God's response when I ask about it is:

"My grace is sufficient."

Okay, God. Let's do this... This morning, I am really appreciating passages in Psalm 18, quoted from *The Message.* (Emphasis mine.)

"I love you, GOD—
You make me STRONG.
God is bedrock under my feet,
the castle in which I live,
my rescuing knight.

My God – the high crag
where I run for dear life,
hiding behind the boulders,
safe in the granite hideout.

I SING to GOD, the Praise-Lofty,
and find myself safe and saved.
***

But me he caught – reached all the way
from sky to sea; he pulled me out
Of that ocean of hate, that enemy chaos,
the void in which I was drowning.
They hit me when I was down,

but GOD stuck by me.
He stood me up on a wide-open field;
I stood there saved – surprised to be loved!

God made my life complete
when I placed all the pieces before him.
When I got my act together,
he gave me a fresh start.
Now I'm alert to GOD's ways;
I don't take God for granted.
Every day I review the ways he works;
I try not to miss a trick.
I feel put back together,
and I'm watching my step.
God rewrote the text of my life
when I opened the book of my heart to his eyes.

I really love that last verse. Sometimes we really need a re-write. A do-over. A mulligan. But He is a God of second chances.

What a God!
His road stretches straight and smooth.
Every God-direction is road-tested.
Everyone who runs toward him MAKES it."

"Everyone who runs toward him, makes it." I am not a runner. In fact, I *LOATHE* running. I find it to be either boring or painful, depending on my level of effort. In the few times I have participated in an organized race, I was often in despair of reaching the finish line. Success was determined by crossing the finish line, and my own success was seriously in doubt. But here, we have success defined, not by crossing the finish line,

but by simply running in the right direction – TOWARDS GOD.
Almost a divine participation trophy! Running ... As opposed to
walking, or standing in the shade, or playing with your phone.

I'm thinking of the stereotypical soap opera scene of the couple
running towards each other in slow motion. *"John!!!"*
"Marsha!!!" [They embrace, background goes to soft focus...
cut scene.]

Jeremiah 31:2-3 in *The Message* comes to mind:

> *This is what the LORD says:*
>
> *"They found grace out in the desert,*
> *these people who survived the killing.*
> *Israel, out looking for a place to rest,*
> *met God out looking for them!" God told them,*
> *"I've never quit loving you, and I never will.*
> *Expect love, love, and more love!"*

Expect love, love, and more love.

100. Lane Closed Ahead

This morning God showed me some things for my own life right
now, which may be true for some of you as well, so I thought I
would share a couple of them.

In one vision, I was driving behind a big black dump truck in
the right lane, minding my own business when it suddenly
braked hard, so I had to do so also. I looked to my left, intending
to pass him, but saw an orange highway construction sign which
read, "Lane Closure Ahead – Merge Left." The left lane was
already full of cars, and traffic was almost stop-and-go in both

lanes. I knew immediately that I was going to be there for a while.

After that, God showed me another vision in which I was driving through a parking lot as a shortcut to the other side, but my way was completely blocked by a truck trying to back a trailer into a parking place. He was "crossing my T" as sailors would say, and I could see a man hurrying up to talk to me. I already knew what he wanted. He was going to ask me to wait while the truck driver did what he needed to do. Again, I knew immediately that I was going to be there for a while.

The two visions had the same message. My life is about to slow down because God is going to have me waiting. Not necessarily specifically for me, but because He is doing something elsewhere, and the road ahead is not ready yet. If I rush ahead, I will definitely be in the way, and I may get in an accident. It is time for me to slow down and *enter the waiting* again. Ugh. Waiting *SUCKS*. I hate it I hate it I hate it I hate it!

I am thinking of the story I read of the Ironman Triathlon in Tahiti. One of the international sports reporters noted the slow pace of life there, and asked the local mayor if they had any word in their language corresponding to the Mexican expression "mañana." (Which means "tomorrow," but it is *INDEFINITE*. As in, *"when I get around to it."*) The mayor was thoughtful for a moment, and then said, "No, we have no word in our language that conveys that great sense of *URGENCY* here."

Ok, tantrum over. Sorry.

Sometimes waiting can feel a lot like being in jail (or in a hospital bed!) You are not allowed to leave and do what *YOU* want to do, because you are compelled to stay right where you are. Meals are provided, but the timing and the selection are totally out of your control. Picky eater? You'll *EAT* it and *LIKE* it! But sometimes, God meets us in jail – in our waiting. Jeremiah 33:1-3 in *The Message* tells us:

> *While Jeremiah WAS STILL LOCKED UP IN JAIL, a second message from GOD was given to him:*
>
> *"This is GOD's Message, the God who made earth, made it livable and lasting, known everywhere as GOD. 'Call to me and I will answer you. I'll tell you marvelous and wondrous things that you could never figure out on your own.' "*

Yeah, I think God doesn't hesitate to put us on ice for a season for his own purposes. And then He meets us in in our jail – in our waiting. Moses spent 40 years tending sheep on the back side of the desert, after fleeing a life of luxury as a prince of Egypt because he killed a man. *FORTY YEARS.* And then he encountered God at the burning bush...

Joseph was 17 years old when God gave him two dreams showing his future status as Prime Minister of Egypt, with his whole family bowing down to him. But he made the mistake of telling them, and shortly after that, his brothers sold him into slavery.

(**Pro Tip**: Not everything God shows you is to be shared! Some things are for you alone. Luke 2:19 in the *NIV* tells us "But Mary treasured up all these things and pondered them in her heart." *The Message* phrases it, "Mary kept all these things to herself, holding them dear, deep within herself." God may be sharing His secrets with you (Amos 3:7) but God may also be saying to you, much like Gandalf to Frodo in *The Lord of the Rings*, "Keep it secret – keep it safe!")

After Joseph was sold into slavery, life became better as a trusted slave of an important man, until he was unjustly thrown in Pharaoh's prison. There he languished. We don't have a record of how long he was slave to Potiphar, or how long he was in prison, but we do know that he was 30 years old when he became Prime Minister. So that's 12 to 13 years of waiting, involuntarily. We don't have any record of his interaction with God during this time, but we are shown that God gives him the interpretation of dreams for two fellow prisoners and then for Pharaoh himself, so Joseph must have had a rich prayer life. But I'm sure he complained to God regularly during those years in waiting about how unfair it all was, not realizing God was setting him up for something.

God spoke to Elijah in his isolation, as he hid from Jezebel in a cave (1 Kings 19). And God had Paul in isolation for three years after his conversion (Galatians 1:11-20) where he was not involved in ministry at all. Peter was in prison (Acts 12) pending trial and execution, when an Angel appeared. His chains fell off, the prison gates opened, and the angel escorted him out to freedom. Paul and Silas were beaten *AND* flogged and left in the stocks in prison in Philippi (Acts 16). God sent an earthquake while they were singing praises, (oh wow!) and all their chains fell off. But unlike Peter, they were not free to leave. Why? Because God had a divine appointment set up for them in that prison cell, just like he had arranged for Joseph in prison, centuries before. It led to the salvation of the warden and his whole family.

Paul obediently went to Jerusalem, knowing he would be arrested there and suffer great hardship. But eventually, he made it to Rome under Roman guard – where he had been wanting to go in the first place! Acts 28:30-31 in *The New International Version* tells us:

> *For two whole years Paul stayed there in his own rented house and welcomed all who came to see him. Boldly and without hindrance he preached the kingdom of God and taught about the Lord Jesus Christ.*

Chuck Colson founded Prison Fellowship after his time in jail, which has impacted countless lives. Tradition tells us the Apostle John (the Revelator) received the book of Revelation, the final book in the Bible, while a prisoner on the Island of Patmos.

So maybe God has you involuntarily waiting right now. Whether in jail, in long-term illness, or maybe stuck in a business with no way out. Maybe, *just maybe,* God has you there for His purposes. I am thinking again of the lyrics to Steven Curtis Chapman's song *Be Still and Know*:

> *Be still and know that He is God*
> *Be still and know that He is Holy*
> *Be still, O restless soul of mine*
> *Bow before the prince of peace*
> *Let the noise and clamor cease*

May God bless you with stillness, and with peace during this slowdown.

101. Um... God?

The oncologist called yesterday, right before my PET scan, and said that the bone marrow results indicated mantle cell lymphoma, a rare and potentially aggressive form of Non-Hodgkin's B-Cell lymphoma. He is referring me to a specialist at MUSC Charleston, the Medical University of South Carolina, and together they will work out a treatment plan. He expects treatment to include Chemotherapy, and perhaps (probably?) bone marrow/stem-cell transplants and some other things I couldn't remember. Which is fine. I trust them to figure it out.

How am I doing? Emotionally good. Physically decent. Symptoms come and go. I started working on a song a few weeks ago, my heart's response to this situation. I finished it last night, and I would like to share it with you. The title is "What Are You Doing, God?" Catchy, right? I'll bet that's a pretty common start to many of our prayers. *"God? Are you there? What are you doing!?!? Why is this happening to me???"* Here's the song:

> *What are you doing, God? I don't understand.*
> *I'm going nowhere fast. You must have a plan.*
> *Why am I here? What is my job?*
> *Why are you keeping me here in the dark?*
> *Do I have a task? What is your plan?*
> *I don't like this waiting. I don't understand,*
> *Why am I here?*

Jesus, I am your servant, You hold me close.
Jesus, You are enough.
Jesus, hold me close and I am safe and warm
In Your Love.

Trouble is coming God. It's part of your plan.
It might be a lonely road, but in your grace I stand.
I know you are here – You're near and not far.
You're right here beside me – here in the dark.
I trust you my God, with all that I am.
Your grace is sufficient, wherever I am.
I'm glad You're here.

Jesus – Light in my Darkness
Jesus – Keeper of Dreams
Jesus – Peace in my Sorrow
As long as I breathe,
I praise Your name

Jesus, I am Your servant –
You hold me close.
Jesus, You are enough.
Jesus, hold me close
and I am safe and warm
In Your Love.
In Your Love.

A year ago, I was in the hospital with Covid. The week before, God told me a trial was coming, and to *"Get Ready."* This same *Get Ready* is resonating now. It's an imperative, not a suggestion. This morning I opened to Jeremiah 12-14 in the *NIV*, and my eyes fell on Jeremiah 12:5.

GOD's Answer:

*If you have raced with men on foot and they
have worn you out, how can you compete with
horses? If you stumble in safe country, how will
you manage in the thickets by the Jordan?*

God was reminding me that I have it easy right now, but it's about to get a lot harder. So pray for me friends. That God will strengthen me and make me ready, and that God will use this for His purposes.

It is well with my soul.

To be continued...

Acknowledgements

Scripture quotations from Chapter 69- The Good Story, are reproduced from First Nations Version: An Indigenous Translation of the New Testament, copyright 2021 by Rain Ministries Inc. Used by permission of InterVarsity Press. All rights reserved worldwide. www.ivpress.com

Scripture Quotations marked The Message are taken from THE MESSAGE, copyright 1993, 2002, 2018 by Eugene H. Peterson. Used by permission of NavPress. All rights reserved. Represented by Tyndale House Publishers.

Scripture Quotations marked NIV are taken from the HOLY BIBLE, NEW INTERNATIONAL VERSION, Copyright 1973, 1978, 1984 by International Bible Society. Used by permission of Zondervan. All rights reserved.

Made in the USA
Middletown, DE
15 January 2024

47890424R00126